MTN MIST MIRAGE +

Marilyn Orlando
14625 Country Lane
Morgan Hill, CA  95037

D0466138

# TEN

## FEET

### TALL,

#### STILL

To Marilyn
Ride on!
Julie Suhr

# TEN
## FEET
### TALL,
#### STILL

*A Personal Odyssey*

*Julie Suhr*

MARINERA PUBLISHING
California

Publisher's Cataloging-in-Publication

Suhr, Julie.
    Ten feet tall, still : a personal odyssey / Julie Suhr.—1st ed.
      p. cm.
    Includes bibliographical references.
    LCCN 201119421
    ISBN 0-9713772-0-0
    1. Suhr, Julie.   2. Horsemen and horsewomen—United States—Biography.   3. Endurance riding (Horsemanship) I. Title.

SF284.52.S84A3   2001               798.23'092
                                      QBI01-701310

Printed in the United States of America

Marinera Publishing
100 Marinera Road
Scotts Valley, CA 95066
USA
Marinera@aol.com

# Table of Contents

# *Dedication*

This story is dedicated to Bob.
He never said "No."

# Acknowledgments

Triumphs are seldom achieved by the efforts of one person, but rather by one person and the support group that surrounds him. My support group has consisted of a family that understood my frailties—and lived with them. My appreciation is unbounded for Bob who joined me and Barbara who shared my need, and for Rob and John who did not understand, but just accepted "this is what Mom does." My sons are seriously and apologetically neglected in this book because it is a horse story and they have not been a part of that side of my life.

I did as told when my neighbor, Marti Ainsworth, an expert with the English language, told me to *"put this story in the first person and get rid of all those clichés!"* Encouragement came from my new found friend, author Rebekah Witter, whose enthusiasm for my unpolished manuscript egged me on and who introduced me to the wisdom of Lynda Paffrath. Lynda, another first time author struggling with the perils of self-publishing, became the soul mate I have never met, but with whom e-mail correspondence has been prolific. Other authors who have traveled a similar path as mine and gave heeded advice include Courtney Hart and Dr. Matthew MacKay-Smith. My heartfelt thanks to Barbara and Rob who, with a great devotion of time, painstakingly checked their mother's spelling, punctuation and grammar. They were gentle in their criticisms and always right. My son John spurred me on by convincing me you can enter uncharted waters (writing a book) and come out on the other bank (seeing it in print) if you swim hard enough. It turned out to be a wide river, and I have emerged somewhat waterlogged, but still paddling and most certainly fulfilled by the experience.

My apologies if there is an over abundance of pictures of myself intermingled with the text. Family albums tend to be self-centered and I hope that in ripping mine apart for this story, I have chosen the right ones to project the message I wanted my readers to discover—that my contributions to the horse world are minimized by what the world of horses has given to me. To help even the score, all profits from the sale of this book will be donated to The American Endurance Ride Conference, Inc. Trails Committee and the Western States Trail Foundation Trails Committee, so that, through trail preservation, others might see the world as I have—from the back of a horse feeling *Ten Feet Tall*.

My appreciation is not limited to my family and friends but extends to those wonderful four-legged creations that educated me, gave me my triumphs, dealt me some failures and stole from my heart when they were lost to me. Their personalities varied as much as those of a roomful of people—the good, the honest, the manipulators, the laggards, those with God given special talents that soared and those of lesser ability that struggled to please a demanding rider.

### the horses that shaped my life—

Andy, a black and white Shetland pony, taught me humility on a
   Thanksgiving Day.
Mignon, a small dun pony of undetermined origin, was to me what
   dolls are to other little girls.
Dick, a grey gelding, awakened in me the thrill of a running horse.

*Jazz*, a chestnut gelding of undetermined age, found life somewhat of a trial, but he plodded through plowed fields because he was asked.

*Sally*, a mustang mare, with her mane blowing in my face, brought me Bob.

*Lady Kay*, a Thoroughbred/saddlebred mare, took a middle aged housewife and returned her to her childhood.

*Chagitai*, a 16 year old Arabian gelding, taught me that animals could experience the pain of homesickness as well as humans.

*\*Marinera*, a Peruvian Paso mare, gave me the wake up call that ignorance was no excuse for abuse and whose forgiveness I needed and was granted. Her indomitable and vibrant spirit demanded and received my admiration.

*Danzarina*, a Peruvian Paso mare, enjoyed pitting her strong will against mine for 27 years. It was a draw. Sometimes she won; sometimes I did.

*HMR Rumadi*, an Arabian gelding, gave me my first endurance win and built my confidence by showing that on one particular day, of the thousands before and to follow, we were the best.

*Beau*, an Arab/Morgan gelding, showed Bob the Tevis Cup Trail, leisurely and at great length.

*SS Myllany*, an Arabian gelding, taught me about not quitting. He was the gutsiest horse I have ever known. His promising career was cut short by an accident.

*SS Riftez*, an Arabian gelding, Myllany's full brother, was an uncomplaining and faithful companion to anyone who climbed upon his back.

*HCC Gazal +/*, an Arabian gelding, is my proud super horse whose excellence put me on the endurance map. Totally without rancor, he never refused a command.

*Lawlifa*, Gazal's mother, brought happiness to all those lucky enough to have one of her 14 foals. At age 25, she introduced a young girl to the wonderful world of horses and trails.

*HCC Rusghala*, an Arabian mare, gave me the honor of being chosen to represent the United States in the 1988 World Championship Ride.

*Eleussa*, an Arabian gelding, was the most obedient horse I have ever known, but his unexpected bucks taught me to never lower my guard. I never quite trusted him.

*Rashina*, an Arabian mare, was neurotic, moody, compulsive. She never learned to like me in the 5,000 miles we shared. But I admired her. She had more innate savvy than most people.

*Rushcreek Q-Ball*, an Arabian mare, who, after one last great performance, was taken from her fan club much too soon.

*T+ Bravo*, an Arabian gelding, gave me back my courage when I had lost my nerve completely.

*Carioco*, a Peruvian Paso stallion. I caressed his body as he took his first breath and, 24 years later, as he took his last.

*Carolana*, a Peruvian Paso mare, was the sweetest tempered and most uncomplaining horse I have ever known. She never stopped giving.

*Khadija*, an Arabian mare, was not prevented by compromised lungs from being the ultimate broodmare, producing sought after foals of quality regardless of sire.

*Fadot*, an Arab/Appaloosa gelding, our gentle giant, went willingly down the trail once his prodigious appetite was satisfied.

*Zayante*, a grade gelding, was probably the best horse I have ridden, but his exuberant antics on the trail forced me to pass him on to younger and more competent riders.

*Springdale Witez*, a Colorado Ranger /Arab gelding, solid and bomb proof, is the kind of horse that keeps old people in the saddle.

*C F War Hymn*, an Arabian gelding, my *Buddy*, keeps me young. His sparkling and smart-aleck personality has given me some of the happiest hours I have ever spent in a saddle.

And finally, to all the good horses in foreign countries that have so willingly carried me upon their backs so that I might view the world from between their ears, my deep and heartfelt gratitude for every step we took together in a world that can be so very beautiful, but that none of us, human or animal, really understand.

*"For the animal shall not be measured by man. In a world older and more complete than ours, they move finished and complete, gifted with extensions of the senses we have lost or never attained, living by voices we shall never hear. They are not brethren, they are not underlings; they are other nations, caught with ourselves in the net of life and time, fellow prisoners of the splendour and travail of the earth."*

The Outermost House by Henry Beston 1888–1968

PROLOGUE

# Around the World in Thirty-five Years

November 1998

Yesterday I completed my 25,000th mile in endurance competition. It was a rainy November day and I spent almost eleven hours in the saddle to acquire the final miles that achieved that long-standing goal—once around the world in competition. How far yet how short when the hours spent on a horse make me a privileged person. I rode a much loved horse. Between us we have 92 years. It was a rewarding day despite the clouds, the rain, the cold and the slippery trails. When that favorite horse trotted out at the end of the ride for the veterinarian inspection with his eyes bright and a spring in his steps, he made me a special person. Achieving a goal brings immense satisfaction, but it also leaves me somewhat nostalgic for the journey that is nearly over, the long, long journey that so enriched my life. This book is about that journey.

I did not embark upon my riding career with a particular goal in mind. But as the years wore on, people asked me repeatedly how long I was going to continue on the trail. Ten years ago I

1

brushed it off with "Oh, either when I'm 75 or reach 25,000 miles—which ever comes last." I really did not dwell on it much until the last several years when problems with my ankles, and warnings from orthopedic surgeons to stop riding, set the goal posts a bit higher than I had planned. It made the triumph a little greater. Having achieved both figures, 75 years and 25,000 miles, I have changed my tune. Now my answer to the question is a simple "As long as I'm still having a good time."

Twenty-five thousand miles is more than once around the globe. For every mile in competition, there have been at least four or five in conditioning and preparation. With thirty-seven years of endurance training and riding behind me, it is a time of reflection. I have been too cold, too hot, too hungry and too thirsty. And I have been scared. I am not a masochist, but really a hedonist because I have done what I wanted to do most. I have finished in the front at rides, in the middle and in the back. I have been humbled and I have stood ten feet tall. I have greeted the dawn from the back of a horse, watched the sun set and the stars appear, and been guided by the moonlight. I have caressed the newborn foals as they drew their first breath and kissed the soft muzzles of old and tired companions as they drew their last. What possesses a 40-year-old woman to want to sit upon horses' backs for thirty-seven years and 150,000 miles?

I do not know the answer. Perhaps it is hidden in the depths of a horse's eye where untold secrets reside—secrets we cannot probe. Or perhaps the die are cast the first time a young girl wraps her arms around a horse's neck and smells the sweetness and feels the warmth.

When I was 8, a pony awakened my love of the animal known as EQUUS. My husband, Bob, compares me to Will Rogers who said he never met a man he didn't like. Bob claims I have never met a horse I didn't like. It is a fairly accurate assessment. My pony preoccupied me as a child and my horses consume my thoughts 69 years later. I have never tired of feeding and caring for them and one of the happiest hours of my day is from 6 to 7 in the morning when I greet their soft nickers with the flakes of hay that start our connection to the new day.

I have lived a privileged life. With marriage and motherhood I thought I had left my first love behind. For twenty years I never rode a horse, or even patted one that I can remember. That part of my life appeared in memory only. But some things lie dormant, not dead. When the responsibilities lessened and my free time expanded, I returned to horses as surely as land and sky meet on a distant horizon. And a whole new world opened, a world I would view from between the ears of many horses as I chased that distant horizon. No picture ever had a prettier frame.

It took me 24 years to get Bob on his first horse. And then the world was mine. From the backs of our horses we have shared the pounding Pacific surf, the Pony Express trail halfway across a nation, the high country of Montana and Wyoming, the Mexican border, the redwood forests of the Northwest, the Shenandoah River of Virginia and the below-sea-level basin of Death Valley. From the backs of horses belonging to others we have seen the Australian Outback, the gorges of the River Tarne in southern France, the Orange Free State and the Drakensberg Mountains of South Africa, the jungle and Mayan ruins of Belize, the Alaskan pipeline from north of the Arctic Circle. We have galloped with the zebras in Kenya and ridden with the reindeer people of Outer Mongolia along the Siberian border. We have cast our shadows alongside those of the Sphinx and of the three Great Pyramids and followed the Nile. We have had our horses chased by Cape buffalo in Botswana and crossed the drought-ridden grasslands of Inner Mongolia on the descendants of the war ponies of Genghis Khan. We have left our footprints on the slopes of the Andes, and on horseback we have gazed at the Mediterranean Sea from sunny Spain. And between the ears of good horses we have viewed the Straits of Magellan near the tip of the South American Continent.

Photographer:
Unknown

The 25,000th Mile
November 1998.

I have never really found much I do not like about horses, but sometimes now a too exuberant one scares me. It happens more frequently than it used to and eventually the day will come when they will be a smaller part of my daily routine. And then I will look back and say "Thank you, God, for making me a privileged person." And I will realize that once around the world is not nearly far enough.

CHAPTER ONE

# The Valley of Heart's Delight

*A horse, a horse, my kingdom for a horse.*

William Shakespeare, Richard III

I cannot remember when I first fell in love with horses. By the time I was 8, indulgent parents had introduced Andy into my life. I learned what it meant to be ten feet tall the first time I sat upon his back. He was a black and white Shetland pony whose entry into my life consumed my thoughts every waking moment.

Andy and I parted ways both figuratively and literally on a Thanksgiving Day. As the turkey roasted, I mounted Andy before the assembled crowd of aunts, uncles, siblings, parents and cousins while wearing my best party dress and new black patent leather shoes. A high-flung unscheduled dismount, the first of many to follow, sent me off to the hospital with two valuable life long lessons. Ponies can hurt you, but humiliation hurts more. As I picked myself up before hovering family members, I watched as one cousin nudged the other and said, "I saw her underpants."

5

The scars of that unfortunate accident are still evident on my chin. Every time I look in a mirror they are there to remind me of the humiliation and shame which accompanied my desire to show off. While they should be a daily reminder to be more careful, they instead remind me that I never saw Andy again. He was banished and off the property overnight. As for the cousin, I never liked her much anyway.

Andy's replacement came in the form of a small aged dun pony of undetermined origin. Her name was Mignon, and it was just easier to festoon her mane and tail with flowers and pampas grass fronds than it was to ask her aged body to carry a child about. And so she was lavished with love and good grooming, which favor she returned by allowing me to cry into her mane when things were not going right in my child's world. This resulted in a maxim of mine—*every little girl should have a mane to cry into when the world is unjust.*

I am not sure at what age she disappeared from my life but it was the start of a long drought during which my horse fantasies had to be derived from reading. I wept over Black Beauty and rode the range with the X Bar X Boys while others my age were reading Little Women and being charmed by Alice In Wonderland.

My home was the Santa Clara Valley, once so aptly referred to as "The Valley of Heart's Delight." It lies south of San Francisco in the fertile valley surrounded by the Santa Cruz Mountains and the Eastern Foothills. It was carpeted with acre upon acre of fruit orchards with blankets of yellow mustard plants beneath their branches. I assume the folklore to be true that Father Junipero Serra dropped mustard seed in the late 1700s as he established the string of missions along the California coast. He believed that each spring the wild mustard plants would return and he and his followers would always be able to find the mission route. The yellow flower did return and in profusion. Two hundred years after Father Serra's journey up the coast, the young children of the Valley of Heart's Delight ran through it with the sheer joy of youth.

My father, Will Weston, grew pears in the dark adobe ground and said there was no richer soil in the world except possibly that which lay east of the Mediterranean in the Fertile Crescent. His orchards in the luxuriant earth of the Santa Clara Valley produced pears that not only were sold locally, but graced the dinner plates of many an exclusive restaurant on the East Coast. He developed markets for his produce in Liverpool and London and was proud of the different varieties which met different needs. The Comice pears were usually shipped fresh under his personal *Old Orchard* label. The Bartletts were used primarily for canning in the local packing sheds and were distributed under the Del Monte label. Others were marketed to baby food manufacturers or sold in the local stores.

My father liked his ranch lifestyle and believed in the golden fruit that was the reward of his hard work. A native Californian who had a strong sense of civic duty, he served on the Santa Clara County Planning Commission for 27 years along with doing other volunteer work. Being chairman of the local draft board during World War II was probably the most difficult. He watched with dismay, but resignation, the post war boom in housing and industry that changed the verdant valley forever. He predicted before others the demise of agriculture in this fertile land, and the "greenbelt" designation he advocated to protect farm property from being annexed by cities and exploited by urban developers is still in existence today.

Education was my father's first priority for his children and he wanted to make certain that they received the best. He was very much an intellectual and his extensive personal library was gathered over the span of many years. A World War I veteran and a survivor of the Great Depression, he was of serious demeanor, and frivolity was not characteristic of him. Standards were to be maintained in the home and in the outside world at all times. He instilled a code of ethics and morality in his children at an early age.

His opposition to my preoccupation with horse activities was the result of his sincere belief in what was right for me. And, in the days when "parents know best," I believed him and suppressed my silent longings. Leisure time was to be filled with improving the mind. I considered myself lucky to have had such a father and do not remember ever resenting his patriarchal approach to family life. When he died at age 87, robbed of most of his vitality, he was ready to go. He had called me 'Sissy' since I was a little girl and his last words to me were, "Be a good girl, Sissy." I have tried.

My mother was the quintessential lady. Of rare beauty, she had a wide circle of friends. I looked up to her and hoped that I could someday emulate her style. She was more sympathetic perhaps than my father in regard to my horse interests, but as he did, she also trod a very straight line.

I never saw my mother leave her bedroom unless fully dressed, bed made and hair in perfect order. To her, it would have been unthinkable to appear in curlers or a housecoat. Her use of profanity never went beyond an occasional "damn" which she uttered quietly under her breath and with apologies to any within hearing distance. She loved to garden and fresh flowers throughout her house were a priority. She set examples of graciousness and expected them to be followed by her two daughters.

Very beloved by her household help, my mother's deep respect for their needs was sincere and fair. When World War II threw our country into one of its most painful periods, she suddenly found herself, perhaps for the first time in her life, without others to help with household chores and daily routines. A large ranch house and three teenagers put demands on her that exceeded what she had experienced in the past. She never missed a step. She cooked and cleaned and washed and ironed without complaint while maintaining her social contacts and civic interests. My mother died at the age of 91 in 1978. Realistically, it was not unexpected, but I have never overcome my loss. I, very simply, adored my mother.

What my parents probably did not realize at the time was that they were instilling in me attributes that in later years would help me in the world I chose for myself, that of an endurance rider. Self-discipline, respect for others and the ability to "see a job through" were traits ingrained in me at an early age by exceptional parents.

My parents, Will and Juliette Weston, set strict standards while providing an Eden for their children.

Andy, the pony that taught me humility on Thanksgiving Day in 1932.

CHAPTER TWO

# Growing Up—Astride and Afoot

*In riding a horse, we borrow freedom.*

Helen Thomsom

In my early years I rode bareback out of necessity more than daring. My second pony, Andy's successor, Mignon, learned quickly to duck under the pear branches in search of the sweet morsels of fruit on the ground. The limbs that just cleared Mignon's back did not favor mine so kindly. After a few scrapes, it became easier for me to forego the saddle and just grab the branch and allow her to continue on without me. As I dropped to the ground, I knew she would not go far because the urge to vary her diet with the juicy pears that had fallen beneath the trees was stronger than her rambling ambitions. She was elderly and in my life for only a few short years. It is with sorrow I have seen this idyllic childhood playground we shared covered by concrete and its name sadly traded from the *Valley of Heart's Delight* to the world-renowned *Silicon Valley*.

The adolescent years came too soon for me and the lack of a

11

horse in my life had to find an outlet in other ways. The great thoroughbred Seasbiscuit was dominating the sporting green, and, to the great distress of my sister, Nancy, I faithfully cut out his pictures and plastered the walls of our shared room with my idol's image. I read horse stories by the dozens and memorized western songs that told of renegade horse that couldn't be ridden. *"Oh that strawberry roan. Oh that strawberry roan. He went up toward the east and came down toward the west. To stay in his middle I 'm doin' my best. Oh that strawberry roan."* I rooted for the wild horses unashamedly in their battle against the men who would destroy their freedom. I sat in my tree house and secretly wrote a book. The title was *BARB WIRE* and told of a captured wild horse who ran through all the fences man erected to deprive him of his freedom. His scarred body was covered with the marks of barb wire and the men who chased him relentlessly always came to no good end. My story's wondrous hero always triumphed as with thundering hooves he reclaimed his rightful position as the head of the wild herd.

I was introduced to hard work during the summers with stints in the packing house and some orchard field work. In the former location I stood on a long platform with four or five other women before three moving belts loaded with pears. As they passed in front, we sorted them according to variety, size and ripeness. Bruised ones went one place, others to the baby food manufacturers, some to the canneries and the Grade A and specialty pears were shipped all over the world. In the field, my pear sorting job consisted of taking the buckets of fruit that the men brought down the ladders and taking the pears one by one and placing them in the fruit boxes that would be collected and taken to the packing sheds. It was not too demanding a job mentally and it helped the time pass if I thought about horses. It put the first earned paychecks in my hands and I diligently saved for the rawhide braided head stall as pictured in a Montgomery Ward catalog and a Navajo blanket of a particularly pleasing design. I didn't have a horse, but I knew that someday I would.

During my horseless days my envy for four cousins, who shared two horses, knew no bounds. When they moved from the country to town, my sister, brother and I inherited their two ancient geldings, Dick and Jazz by name. Life was truly worth living again and they brought me untold hours of joy. Neither my sister, Nancy, nor my brother, Bill, had the interest in them that I did. The two horses virtually became mine alone and, at my hands, they never suffered neglect. Riding instructions were nonexistent in my life. Trial and error and an intense interest taught me almost everything I know about horses even to this day. My riding trails were up one row of pear trees and down the next and I never seemed to tire of it as I made paths through the yellow mustard that often rose above my horses' knees. An occasional jack rabbit, alarmed at the intrusion in his world, would flee in great leaping bounds and startle my horse and awake me from whatever reverie I was lost in at that moment.

Jazz in 1938.

Photo by:
Berton Crandall

Dick in 1938. He taught me the thrill of a running horse.

Dick gave me my first introduction to the elation of speed—the speed of a running horse. It was a stunning experience for me. He was quite controllable leaving the barn. Once turned around for the homeward trip, however, his speed increased beyond my abilities to control. My survival instinct told me to pull back on the reins and slow this out of control horse, but my desire for the thrill told me to urge him on even faster. Childhood dreams raced through my mind as I won the Kentucky Derby, the Grand National and that race through the pear trees and mustard fields with an imaginary opponent. Even the mighty Seabiscuit would have met his match.

Jazz taught me patience. In retrospect, I think Jazz probably ached, or perhaps he was just very old, but he was a noble beast that trudged placidly through the plowed fields. The heel nudges in the ribs that would send Dick racing had little or no effect on Jazz and so I finally gave up and let him determine the speed. I had no near neighbors or anyone in the family who shared my horse interest so most of my riding was solitary, but I did not mind. My German shepherd dog, Fling, followed at the horses' heels. His companionship and that of the horses was all that I needed. Living in the country denied me the friendships that are forged by having many neighbors but I would not have traded places with any of my city living school classmates.

Riding in the moonlight treated me to all sorts of mysterious fantasies, but night riding was not condoned by my parents. Certain of being denied permission if requested, I skipped the formality and, upon occasion, snuck silently out of the house once everyone was asleep. The stairs outside my second floor bedroom door squeaked, and fearful that I would awaken somebody if I used that avenue of escape in the middle of the night, I chose a different route. From the second-floor balcony outside my bedroom door, I could hop up to the adjacent attic roof, hunch my way across it and drop to a garage roof and then to a garden shed. A short jump down and I was on my way to the barn. Once there, I bridled my horse and put a halter on the second horse so that he could be led. If only one horse was taken out of the corral, the other would whinny frantically for his lost companion and most likely awaken someone. Fling, in his anticipation over a midnight romp, barked with delight and enthusiasm but was quickly hushed. Then it was up and down the pear tree rows in the moonlight and along the borders of a hayfield where the crickets filled the night air with their summertime songs. To this day, I consider it the most beautiful music in the world and it never fails to take me back nostalgically to an idyllic childhood.

Storm clouds were gathering, however. My father became increasingly distressed about a daughter whose sole reason for being seemed to be horses to the exclusion of mental acquisitiveness in other fields. Much the intellectual himself, he believed, and probably quite rightfully, that my narrow interests needed broadening. It was suggested that I attend a preparatory school in New England where my grandmother had studied many years before. I did not want to leave everything I loved for the new and unfamiliar, but my parents had made it abundantly clear what was expected of me. I loved them and pleasing them was important to me. The decision was made. I remember to this day my father's parting words as he stood on the train platform waving goodbye: "Get the horses out of your system." It was a forlorn journey for how would Dick, Jazz and my dog, Fling, cope without my daily attention? I fortunately did not know that I had hugged and caressed them all for the last time.

My mother traveled with me. As we left the Pacific Coast farther behind, the great American Desert of Nevada and Utah unfolded beyond the train windows, a large part of which I would someday cross on a horse on the Pony Express Trail. I was not a very good traveling companion because for the first time in my life I knew genuine unhappiness. The cornfields of the Midwest gave way to the more industrialized parts of the nation and I watched them pass, but with little interest. We took a side trip to Washington, D.C. where our local Congressman, fellow pear grower Jack Z. Anderson, showed us the United States Senate Chambers, the House of Representatives and the Supreme Court. We stood at the base of the Lincoln Memorial and the first true waves of patriotism swept over me. My memories of that awakening are profound and lasting. My parents were correct. I needed an introduction to a world outside of the plowed fields, the smell of fruit trees in bloom and a Valley of Heart's Delight.

We arrived at the all-girl boarding school in Andover, Massachusetts. My father, who believed strongly that the greatest gift he could give his children was a good education, had done what he thought was best for me. But my mother sensed my sadness and, after getting me settled in my new school, signed me up for some trail rides at a local stable. I do not know whether she ever told my father. I was introduced to English saddles, jodhpurs and mount-

Headed for Boarding School on the East Coast, September 1941.

ing blocks which were a far cry from my previous bareback rides in old blue jeans and the running jump that put me astride. Riding among the fall colors of New England was the only bright spot of that year. It was the hardest time of my life and with great immaturity, I spent a lot of time being unhappy. I once sent an eight year old son off to summer camp for a week. His only letter home was three sentences long—concise and to the point. "I hate it here. I cry a lot. My pillow is wet." Apparently he had learned well at his mother's knee. In Massachusetts, 20 years before, there was also a wet pillow. Other than losing a loved one, I have never known any pain greater than that of homesickness.

A tradition of the school was to have the students take turns giving reports on current events as gleaned from Boston newspapers. It constituted a part of our History and English grades. The war in Europe was in full sway on December 6, 1941 when it was my turn to present the news, which primarily concerned the Japanese ambassadors who were visiting with President Roosevelt in Washington, D.C. It was a miserable experience for me and talking before a roomful of people, including my teachers, was difficult. The next day the Japanese bombed Pearl Harbor and the following day war was formally declared. Our lives were changed forever.

My mother's almost daily letters were a source of comfort to me, but the news not always so. The Boston papers told of the unmanned incendiary balloons being sent by the Japanese across the Pacific to set the forests of the Northwest ablaze. They didn't succeed, but the threat was real. United States warplanes were dispatched over the ocean to intercept them and shoot them out of the skies before they reached our mainland. A Japanese submarine hurled shells at the Santa Barbara coast and, again, no damage occurred, but the memory of the attack on Pearl Harbor was very fresh and residents of the West Coast were rightfully frightened. My family wrote of the blackout curtains they made, which had to be in place before they could turn on any house lights. My homesickness, which I hid from my family, became deeper and it was a somber time, not only for me, but the world at large.

Back in Massachusetts, the school principal told us in an assembly that we must carry on as normally as possible. But the morning papers and the news from home told me otherwise. As with most students, visiting the school principal under my own initiative was not something I did easily, but I boldly approached her and said we should be making a contribution to the war effort. She was a nice woman but I could tell she did not have the slightest idea what to do with me. She solved her dilemma by locating some burlap sacks and telling me to fill sandbags and place them around the base of my dormitory. It was somewhat rewarding for the first hour, but after that it was drudgery and my erstwhile good friends, who had entered upon the project with enthusiasm, faded more rapidly than even I did. The seemingly endless school year dragged on.

# CHAPTER THREE

# *Of College and Free Balloons*

*Allow them not to gallop in swirling floods,*
*but let them graze in glades by brimming streams.*

Virgil

When I returned home to California in June, Dick and Jazz had gone to greener pastures and my beloved Fling had been killed by an auto on Bayshore Highway which, by right of eminent domain, had bisected my father's orchards in the 1930s. War rationing was in full swing and gas, shoes and meat products were bought only after the proper stamps were presented. My father was chairman of the local draft board, a job he never liked but took out of civic duty. Deciding which local boys would go off to fight and who would be deferred preyed on his mind. He empathized with the pleading fathers and the hand-wringing mothers for he also had a son approaching draft age, my brother Bill. As far as I was concerned, the message from my family was clear. You are going to college now and you will not be riding horses anymore.

Four years at Stanford University were marred slightly by a D

19

in Creative Writing, which is the reason this book was not written a long time ago. It was my only D and I graduated on schedule with a degree in political science. I studied intently the first year because I seriously doubted my ability to compete in the classroom with my fellow students who all seemed to have been student body presidents, editors of their high school yearbooks and quarterbacks on football teams. Then an active social life intervened and I learned the art of coasting along just well enough to pass, not an academic intellectual but a reasonably conscientious student.

I made a few minor contributions to the war effort. Rolling bandages[1] for the Red Cross and selling war bonds out of an Army tank parked on the main street of Palo Alto occupied some of my free time. As boys I knew gave up their education in order to fight, I realized that some would not return and it weighed on my conscience. We were told to "write letters to our boys" to keep up their morale and it turned me into a prolific letter writer. I was never sure if telling a boy in a trench of the good times at home did much for his morale, but I was not much of a deep thinker and accepted what I had been asked to do. Football games had been suspended and replaced with war bond rallies and marching Army Special-

Selling war bonds from an Army tank in 1944, Palo Alto, CA.

ized Training Program units on campus. On the West Coast the details of the Bataan Death March and fighting in the South Pacific took precedence over the war in Europe. It was not a good time for the world, but my 18-year-old outlook on life was generally optimistic after my return to California. My privileged and protected existence had insulated me somewhat from the wartime brutalities being committed in the world beyond my Valley of Heart's Delight.

My life changed somewhat when a young man, who shared my Santa Clara Valley upbringing on a neighboring ranch, was called to service. When George Brown went off to fight the war in the South Pacific as a P-51 fighter pilot, he asked me to care for a buckskin mare he bought as she went through town in a boxcar loaded with wild horses headed for slaughter. The $50 purchase price included a saddle and bridle. He called her Sally and she had an overwhelming desire to run every place full tilt. If she ran fast enough, her elegant long black mane blew in my face and life was good. I was still riding bareback and I did not count the number of times I fell off that summer, but I am sure it was in double digits. It did not take Sally long to learn that a sudden application of the brakes or a quick sideways turn would deposit me upon the ground. The fields of yellow mustard were good to me once more, softening the falls, and minor bruises were the only consequences. To her credit, Sally usually stood by, looking quite pleased with herself, and waited for me to grasp her thick black mane and pull myself once more upon her back. I was riding again and could ask no more. Besides, Sally's sturdy legs would carry me to new adventures.

During the war, Moffett Field, about five miles east of Stanford and five miles northwest of my home, was an active wartime military base. The U.S. Navy made it one of the headquarters for their Lighter Than Air Fleet. The blimps were used to patrol off the shore along the West Coast from the Canadian border to that of Mexico to prevent enemy submarine infiltration. Because their large surface made them subject to the vagaries of the wind if their engines failed, their pilots had to take "free balloon" training in order to better understand wind currents. A free balloon consisted of a large helium-filled bag with a wicker basket suspended below. In the basket would be four to six naval officers and other personnel. When they wanted to go up, they emptied sand bags over the side; when they wanted to descend, they valved (or released) helium. Changing altitudes to catch the prevailing winds gave them some control over their direction. The theory was that if the blimps ever lost engine power, this training would pay off. I lived downwind from Moffett Field and the wind currents usually sent the balloons in my direction.

Sally and I became experts at balloon-chasing. The top of my father's tank house was a good place to check the direction the wind was blowing, and to determine which way the balloons were going that day. Then my borrowed mustang mare and I would depart in that direction on our hunting foray. The Santa Clara Valley at that time was still primarily agricultural and there were very few fences to bar us in our pursuit. Sooner or later the balloons had to come down in whatever open area they chose and Sally and I were frequently there to greet them.

There certainly must have been more subtle ways of meeting men, but having strangers fall out of the skies at my horse's feet was at least novel. For one balloon occupant the day delivered some unexpected surprises. Not only did Robert Suhr's balloon go through some high tension wires and set a neighboring hay field ablaze, but it landed so rapidly that the person standing next to him broke his leg when he failed to grasp the guy rope and suspend his weight upon touchdown with Mother Earth. When the balloon finally settled to the ground, Ensign Suhr was met by a girl on horseback. Sally and I had caught our prey and for that I shall be ever grateful to my neighbor, George, for loaning me this $50 mustang—this little mare whose mane blew in my face when she ran.

U.S. Navy free balloon, summer 1944.

U.S. Navy free balloon, 1944.

Sally

Bob was stationed in Tillamook, Oregon with occasional temporary assignments at Moffett Field. Upon his graduation from college, the war in Europe was in full swing and he entered the Navy to participate in the V-5 program, which was flight training to become a naval aviator. He transferred from heavier-than-air aircraft to lighter-than-air aircraft after his basic training. He was quite dashing in his uniform and his presence in my life remedied the dearth of males on the wartime Stanford campus. I became pretty preoccupied with him. In 1945, the dropping of the atom bomb on Japan brought the war to a halt. Bob was free to withdraw from the Navy, but remained another year waiting for me to finish my fourth year at college so that I could fulfill my promise to my father that I would graduate.

We were married two weeks after I received my Stanford degree. It was 1946 and the awful war that had occupied our thoughts and changed our lives, at long last, had ended in victory. We journeyed north up the coasts of California, Oregon and Washington and then into British Columbia. We had a new Ford coupe and gas rationing was over. Bob had $1400 in Navy terminal leave pay and we were carefree and in love as we drove from Vancouver up the Revelstoke Highway where in one entire day of driving we saw not a single other car. The Trans-Canadian Highway, which had been closed during the war, had been regraded and open for less than two weeks. The Rockies were impressive and the moose in the road and lumberjack pancakes at Salmon Arm were all duly noted in a honeymoon diary.

Beer at the local pubs was 10 percent alcohol and cost a dime, but local regulations insisted that men and women be served alcohol only in separate quarters. We spent five days in Banff and Lake Louise and then continued our journey across Canada. We did not plan well, as Indian Days in Banff were starting the day we left and the Calgary Stampede was over the day we arrived in that town. But I was a married woman now and not thinking of horses. Those days were gone. Youthful passions were left behind as I entered upon a new life with all the anticipation and excitement of a new bride.

We journeyed across the great prairie states of Canada and then on to Niagara Falls. From this traditional honeymoon spot, we dropped back into the United States and headed for Bob's hometown of Norwalk, Ohio. We spent the rest of the summer living with his family and working in their summer store on the shore of Lake Erie. At the end of the summer we headed back to California.

When we returned from our honeymoon, my small corral had been torn down and the barn turned into a tool shed. The hayloft and Dick and Jazz's two tie stalls were no more. My query to my father was answered with, "You are a married woman. You will never ride a horse again." And I believed him.

For twenty years I never rode a horse, or even patted one that I can remember. Four babies in six years, and the starting of a business occupied our energies. With Bob as the driving force, and me fulfilling the role of an unskilled secretary, he started his own insurance agency in our small living-dining-bedroom. When the cat had kittens on his files in the linen closet, he moved to an office in town with a paid secretary and I became a full-time mother. I was totally happy in my role and horses became a part of my past and engaged little of my thoughts.

With three children to raise, and working hard to overcome the loss of another in infancy, I threw myself willingly into community activities. I became active in women's organizations, helped the PTA, warmed Little League benches for eleven years, chaired a Santa Clara County Mothers March of Dimes effort, canvassed the block for cancer research funds, chauffeured the Girl Scouts, wrote a newsletter for the local Goodwill chapter, and helped with fund-raising events for different organizations.

Bob was even more active in the community. His business had grown and the family's needs were being met. He became politically active both locally and on a larger scale. He devoted time to local tax associations and was a successful fund raiser for community projects along with serving on many boards. It struck me how much he was like my father, who believed sincerely that one should give back to a community as much as possible by volunteer work. My horseless existence was fulfilling and we watched with pleasure as our children grew to adulthood with a minimum number of family crises.

A chance encounter with an older friend resulted in an invitation to go riding in 1962. I accepted, and, as an alcoholic slips from grace, I knew within the first half mile that horses would play a part in my future. It had been two decades since I had felt ten feet tall, but the love had lain dormant, not dead. After a year of riding the friend's horse, I wanted my own mount. We lived in town where it was impossible to keep a horse, but a place to board one was found in the Almaden Valley. That discovery was closely followed by the purchase of a half thoroughbred mare whose name was Lady Kay. She brought me untold hours of happiness and once again I trod the fields of yellow mustard, this time in the Almaden Valley.

I found it possible to serve breakfast to Bob and the children and, as soon as they disappeared for work and school, be out the door headed for "my" horse. I timed my return to be back before being missed. Wishing them to think my day had been spent slaving over household chores rather then hedonistic pursuits, I frequently turned the washing machine on just before they came in the door to further the impression. A friend of mine sprays Lemon Pledge by the front door just before her husband arrives to give him a similar impression. She also has a horse

My rides were primarily alone as they had been in my youth, but occasionally spent with a good companion, June Matthewson, who had introduced me to Lady Kay and trail riding. The explorations of the hills around the Almaden Golf Course, so different from the pear trees rows of earlier days, were days of discovery. The return to my childhood love was complete. In truth, the child had never grown up. Nor has she to this day.

CHAPTER FOUR

# Introduction to Endurance Riding

*I used to be a pleasure rider, but,*
*Since discovering endurance,*
*I no longer ride for pleasure.*
*I ride for the bliss.*

Joyce Kellenberger, endurance rider, 1997

My addictive behavior started with a chance remark by my friend, June, who had sold me Lady Kay. She had heard of a ride in the Sierra Nevada where you rode all day and all night—for a hundred miles even! What, thought I, could be more fun than that? The term "endurance riding" wasn't in anybody's vocabulary and it sounded as though some congenial horse-loving people were having a good time riding through the mountains. If you completed the ride successfully within a twenty-four hour maximum time limit you were awarded a lovely sterling silver buckle emblazoned with a raised Pony Express rider dashing across the prairie. I really wanted one of those buckles!

I called for information and was told by Wendell Robie, the

27

founder of the 100 Mile One-Day Western States Trail Ride (more commonly called the Tevis Cup Ride), that the way to prepare was to keep your horse lean and to have a saddle blanket, wet from a day's workout, in the tack room each night. Fair enough. So, with great zeal, I underfed and under-trained. A physically unconditioned horse sweats rather easily so once the saddle pad was damp, I figured I was following Wendell's orders and returned to the barn. I launched myself into the project of getting a horse ready to go a hundred miles in one day with total abandon and not one whit of good sense. When the appointed time for this unwise endeavor on my part arrived, we borrowed a pickup truck from my brother, Bill. We then rented a horse trailer for Lady Kay and added three children and the family dog to the entourage. I set off to conquer the backbone of the Sierra Nevada on a horse trained primarily around a golf course. I bought a new pair of jeans so I would look nice for the people and, as the waves lapped at the shores of Lake Tahoe, I climbed upon Lady Kay, and departed in the 5 A.M. darkness of a Saturday morning in mid-July. The husband, the children and the dog drove off to Auburn, never doubting that they would see me arrive in due course at the Fairgrounds a hundred miles away.

It was then the eighth running of the Tevis Cup Ride and there were 56 entries. Lady Kay and I were 56th arriving at Robinson Flat, the first veterinarian checkpoint, where the horses were examined to determine their degree of fitness to continue. The seams of the new jeans had rubbed my legs raw; Lady Kay, plundered by my ignorance, had a pulse rate far above the mandatory recovery rate of 72 beats per minute; her respiration was elevated and she was lame. Her problems, thankfully, were short-lived, and very much shorter than my disappointment. Bob, the children and the dog waited at the finish line in vain while halfway up the mountain I, physically exhausted and emotionally beaten, was returning to my childhood by crying into my horse's mane. So ended my adventurous folly. I returned home with deferred

Photo by:
   Charles Barieau

Julie Suhr and Lady Kay with Wendell Robie, 1964.

dreams and was met by my mother's pronouncement that she knew I would "never be that foolish again."

But my heart told me otherwise. I had tried and failed, but the exhilaration of just being a participant in that ride lingered. For someone who had never ridden in rugged mountains, the high country called me and I knew I would return. The early rides among the rows of pear trees in my Valley of Heart's Delight were being replaced in my heart with the call of the High Sierra.

Back in Auburn, Wendell Robie's faithful ride secretary, Dru Barner, felt pitifully sorry for me because she had trouble believing that anybody could be so naive as to come as ill prepared to the Tevis Cup Ride as I had in 1964. So she called one day and offered me Chagatai, a 16-year-old Arabian gelding, for the following year's ride. Dru had ridden Chag for many years and won the Tevis Cup on him in 1961. Now she wanted a faster mount, but she felt her aging horse would get me to the finish line within the twenty-four allotted hours and I would be able to claim the silver buckle that had evaded me in my first effort.

Once again renting a trailer, we transported Chagatai (named after a son of Genghis Khan) to Saratoga where we now lived and put him in a boarding stable nearby. This time my approach to training a horse was a little more realistic than the jaunts around a golf course with Lady Kay. I knew now what to expect, not just for the horse but for myself. But I did not find my borrowed horse par-

Photo by: Charles Barieau

Dru Barner and Chagitai, 1964.

ticularly inspiring on the local trails. I kept searching but never saw the "look of eagles" in his eyes that Dru so dramatically described and which she claimed made him great. He just seemed to me to be a pretty average horse and I was puzzled about his many triumphs over the Tevis Cup Trail.

The answer came very quickly when I returned to the Sierra Nevada Mountains to make my second attempt at conquering 100 miles on horseback. Unloaded from the trailer, Chag's head went up and his neck arched. He looked about, inhaled deeply and sent out a bugle call. He was home where he belonged! My homesick days on the east coast returned. As with me then, Chagatai had been homesick.

Chag's home for many years had been a fenced corral and barn within 500 feet of the finish line of the Tevis Cup Ride. His life had been spent on these trails. When he was trailered to Lake Tahoe for the start of the event, he knew exactly what his job was the next day. He was supposed to go home to Auburn. And that is exactly what he did. I hung on while he coursed his way from the Lake to Squaw Valley, climbed the mountains and descended into the deep canyons and forged the streams with the storied look of eagles shining brightly in his eyes. Every mile of the trail had been his private playground since his birth. His confidence in attacking it gave me the confidence I needed so badly.

The route was changed somewhat that year because a heavy snow pack in the Sierra had swollen the American River to the point that it was impossible to cross on horseback. A circuitous detour led us through some open fields of tall golden oats. The moon was full and the crickets filled the air with the musical chorus I had loved as a child. Memories of my nightly excursions with Dick and Jazz, so many years before, returned and I was wondrously happy.

Chag met the veterinarian parameters easily and there was never any doubt about his fitness to continue. I was wearing my oldest and softest pair of jeans and my legs remained unblem-

Photo by: Charles Barieau
TEVIS CUP buckle.

ished from the chafing and discomfort I had known with Lady Kay and the new jeans a year earlier. When I arrived at the finish line I was, after a long hiatus, ten feet tall once again. The husband, the children and the dog welcomed me triumphantly. It did not matter that two thirds of the riders had finished before I had— no one's personal achievement could surpass the tumult of joy I felt. I needed no mane to cry into this time. I knew that I could spend the rest of my life reflecting on this one glorious day. This time my mother said, "I am so glad that you have that behind you. Now you can go on to other things."

I returned Chagatai to Dru, and went back to riding Lady Kay who, I realized now, was ill-suited for endurance riding. Having no other options, I was content. Well, for a while anyway. I mean, after all, I had that elusive silver buckle. I finally moved it from under my pillow and put it on my belt where I was sure it looked very splendid to anyone casting an eye my way, even if they seemed reticent in mentioning it.

When I returned home, I mused daily on the ride. I felt that there had been more than a buckle gained by my participation. Being a part of the Tevis Cup Ride had been one of the greatest privileges of my life. This ride over the Western States Trail had allowed me to challenge myself and fail, and then to try again and succeed. As with other riders I met, those that fall short the first time usually return and clear the mountain hurdle that had tripped them up previously. The emotional rewards are great and the highs and lows of training a horse to whip this inspiring trail are all worthwhile even if the finish line is never found. I also made a personal commitment. My memories of this ride would remain forever, but my dreams for the future would overwhelm them.

Photo by: Charles Barieau

In 1969 a horse slipped off the Tevis Cup Trail and had to be rescued by a U.S. Army helicopter. He suffered no injuries.

# How a 100-mile endurance race is run

**START**
There are two types of starts — controlled and shotgun. In a controlled start, a rider guides the pack at a controlled pace for about a mile, then lets them go. Shotgun starts are mad dashes from the starting line.

**FINISH**
Reaching the finish line first does not guarantee victory. Horses must pass a postride check 30-60 minutes after crossing the line. An overridden, exhausted horse can be eliminated by the veterinarian — even if it comes in first. The goal is to complete the ride on a healthy, sound horse.

**First vet check**
Vet checks usually are 12-15 miles apart. The first check is often a "gate" check — horses are allowed to continue as soon as they meet recovery (pulse and respiration) guidelines. This allows better-conditioned horses to move immediately to the front of the pack.

**Second vet check**
Horses coming into check areas must meet recovery criteria and wait a mandatory rest period, from 10-60 minutes, depending on race conditions.

**Seventh vet check**
The final series is crucial to the front-runners. A fast pace might increase a lead but could cause trouble if the horse reaches the check in bad shape.

**Third vet check**
Pit crews tend to the increasing stress on both horse and rider. Horses are sponged with cool water and allowed to drink and eat. Electrolytes and other supplements may be administered.

**Sixth vet check**
It is now dusk, and pit crews must prepare helmet lights and other illumination gear for the riders.

**Fifth vet check**
At the 65-mile point, stress is increasing rapidly. Veterinarians might require extended rest for the horse.

**Halfway check and break**
In some 100-mile rides, a mandatory vet check and one-hour rest period comes at this point. Saddle and tack are removed and the horse is allowed to drink and eat. Riders eat lunch while pit crews tend to the horse. Shoes are checked, sore muscles are massaged and strategy discussed.

By Bob Laird, USA TODAY

## What vets check

Pit crew may sponge the animal with water to lower body temperature and allow pulse level to fall. When ready to be examined, they yell out, "P and R!" (pulse and respiration). Race vets then use several methods to gauge horse's health:

▶ **Pulse recovery:** Horse must regain a predetermined rate. In humid areas, the rate might be as high as 72 beats a minute or as low as 60 in cooler climes.

▶ **Respiration:** Breathing rate is observed by watching horse's chest or listening with stethoscope. Criteria is usually about 40 breaths a minute.

▶ **Other measurements:** Vets might require that a horse's temperature be taken if overheating is suspected. Rider also might be asked to trot the horse unmounted to look for soundness problems.

Source: USA TODAY research

USA TODAY, Thursday, March 21, 1991.

CHAPTER FIVE

# In the Beginning

*Much of the world views horses as a replaceable commodity. I view them as irreplaceable treasures.*

Mike Sofen, 1997

The Tevis Cup Ride starts south of Truckee, California and ends one hundred miles west above the American River Canyon in the Gold Rush town of Auburn. The rider and his horse are allowed 24 hours to complete the course—24 hours in which the world will make one great revolution and the sun will have gone full circle from dawn to high noon, from high noon to dusk, from dusk to the dark of midnight and then from midnight to the next dawn. A tedious journey? Not at all. A rare privilege.

They say that man learns from the hardships of his forefathers. What a learning process the Tevis Cup Ride is. The history of the West is there in the trails carved out of the canyon walls by the footsteps of the horses and mules that carried men in search of gold into the mountains and out again with their precious nuggets. It is there in the few remaining buildings in towns such as Michigan Bluff, where Leland Stanford's first store still stands. It is there in the hydraulic tailings that scarred the once unblemished mountainsides a hundred and fifty years ago—before the computer, nuclear energy and two World Wars. Before the internal combustion machine, the electric light bulb, instant communications and Silicon Valley. And before the Tevis Cup Ride. It is there in the American River, which still flows over the same boulders and makes the same graceful flowing turns that it has for hundreds, perhaps thousands, of years.

We who have a love of trail riding have the benefit of being a part of this history. The same energy depleting and unrelenting sun that seared the miners and their animals in the 1840s sears the horses and riders of today. The rivers and streams offer the same renewal to hot and parched throats of both man and beast. The boulder fields at the 7,000 and 8,000-foot level that slowed those early adventurers, slow the current trespassers of this pristine area. The view from the high country toward the hills of Auburn, one hundred miles away, is the same vista upon which our predecessors gazed. We are literally tramping in their footsteps and we can identify with them and feel a closeness. Their past has become our present.

The modern-day concept of riding 100 miles in one day must be credited to Wendell Robie, an Auburn, California lumber and business man whose passion for his beloved gold country and Arabian horses combined with an unusual zest for life. Wendell Robie was not your ordinary man or your ordinary horseman. I will never forget my first introduction because it was indelibly imprinted on my hand by his hand-shake. His outstretched hand and booming voice spoke of warmth and friendliness. The grip, which might go on for as long as ten seconds, was bone-crushing, especially if you wore a ring.

The first ride with Wendell was usually memorable also. He was totally in command. At the front, regardless of the size of the group, he and his horses conquered the Auburn hills with gusto and with his faithful followers hanging on for dear life and not daring to ask for a short breather. One rider commented that she did not think Wendell considered it a good ride unless there was a crisis. He usually found one. If not, he could manufacture one. The challenge of the mountains was to conquer them and the more adversity encountered, the greater Wendell's victory. I was touched by the fact that he always called me "honey," a term of endearment, I foolishly thought. My awakening came when I read in his biography that he always called women whose names he could not remember "honey."

But to get on with his story, this Auburn lumberman, business-man, town mover and shaker, was an ardent horseman whose respect and pride in his Arabian horses was boundless. Folklore has it that someone bet Wendell that horses today were not as good as yesteryears'. Wendell was incapable of letting such a provocative statement remain unchallenged and so he replied that his horse could go a hundred miles in one day. The man said it could not be done. If someone told Wendell it could not be done, it was done. It is more likely, however, that the following exchange between Wendell and a man from Montana, that took place on the pages of the Western Horseman magazine in 1950 and 1951, was the real catalyst that has resulted in thousands playing the toughest game in town—The Tevis Cup Ride. It was Bill Stewart of Miles City, Montana who hurled the challenge that Wendell could not resist.

The February 1950 issue of Western Horseman printed the following letter in a column titled LETTERS FROM RIDERS

The Challenge

Western Horseman:

In John Richards Young's article "The Arab Horse Speaks for Himself" . . . (Dec. 1949) Dr. George H. Conn, of Freeport, Ill. states, that the Arabian is the horse that has all the world's records for distance performance. I do not believe that is true as I rode Drifter, a Thoroughbred gelding, 81 miles in seven hours and 10 minutes and 27 seconds. A year later I rode the same horse 127 miles (from Hill

Creek to Miles City) in 12 hours and 10 minutes and 36 seconds. These times were officially clocked by three judges and I haven't heard of any other horse accomplishing the same distance or even 50 miles at that speed an hour. I also challenge Dr. Conn, Carl Raswan or any other Arab enthusiast to an endurance race any distance from 50 to 200 miles for money, marbles or chalk.

(s) Bill Stewart
Miles City, Montana

## THE CHALLENGE IS ACCEPTED
*Western Horseman,* March 1950

Western Horseman:

In your February issue, the first item in your Letters from Riders department is a 50 to 200 mile endurance race challenge to any Arabian horse owner for money, marbles or chalk by one Bill Stewart. I accept this challenge and being the challenged party, I select the Auburn-Lake Tahoe horse trail in California for the race at any date during the next summer which will be to Mr. Stewart's convenience. The distance is 90 miles and, in view of Mr. Stewart's astonishing records over long distances, it is hoped that he will not consider this too short.

However, since the 90 miles of this horse trail climbs and crosses the crest of the Sierra Nevada, he may find it ride enough. This is a direct west to east trail starting at elevation 1400, crosses the Sierra in Squaw Pass at 8600 feet, and drops to Lake Tahoe at 6225. From Auburn to Lake Tahoe this trail is on a natural footing of dirt and mountain rock. It is selected by reason of being a California trail—removed and free from oil surfaced automobile road travel. I will bet $250 on my horse Bandos AHRC 1785 by Nasr from Baida, against the chalk, marbles or equal money on Stewart's horse Drifter. Each horse shall carry equal weight and I would like a minimum of 165 pounds.

While calling this gentleman on his challenge, I do not want to be considered as using it to name my horse as champion to represent Arabian horses. There are so many good horses, but Stewart wanted an endurance race of distance he named from any Arab owner, and so he can have it.

(s) Wendell Robie, Box 1228, Auburn, Calif.

STAND OFF
> *Western Horseman,* October 1950.

Our readers will remember the letter from Bill Stewart which appeared in the February 1950 issue in this section in which he challenged "... any Arab enthusiast to an endurance race, the distance
from 50 to 200 miles for money, marble or chalk". In the March issue
this challenge was accepted by Wendell Robie, and, so we thought,
the race was on. Since the letter carried in the June issue, we have
heard nothing from either party. *WESTERN HORSEMAN* sent the
following letter to Mr. Stewart with a copy to Mr. Robie, and we are
quoting——

Dear Mr. Stewart,
Quite a few of our readers have been inquiring as to the status of
   the race on which Mr. Robie accepted your challenge.
Since the acceptance of the challenge carried in this magazine, we
   would like to keep our readers posted on it and would appreciate
   any any information you have.
We would like to know the place the race will take place, the start
   date, ending and other details.
We are sending a copy of this letter to Mr. Robie and sincerely hope
   that you will give us the information at an early date
   (s) "The Western Horseman"

WE'RE READY
ENDURANCE RACE STATUS from *Western Horseman*
(date unreadable)

Here is the latest news we have on the proposed race between
Wendell Robie and Bill Stewart (Letters from Riders, March 1950)
We are quoting from two letters written by Mr. Robie and addressed
to The Western Horseman and Bill Stewart.

> *Western Horseman,* Saturday, March 14

I had a letter from Bill Stewart, the young man from Montana and
hurriedly hand-wrote a reply in order not to keep him waiting. This
copy is for your information.
   It indicates what he wrote about. It does not show if he intends to

get something settled definitely or if he will try to set some newly changed location conditions which I may not be able to meet. While my job of earning a living and improving a brush and timber ranch can give a day of this summer for this race as accepted, it won't pan out a week to trailer off someplace else. This, I reckon, is my fault for not learning how to handle work differently or not working.

(s) Wendell Robie

Dear Mr. Stewart:

I just came in this morning from the redwood country up on the northwest coast and hasten to answer your letter which arrived here yesterday. In it is a note that you want to place the endurance race of your horse with mine at Miles City or Colorado or Idaho and you suggest the purse should be $1500. In another place, you might consider the race in California over the Auburn-Lake Tahoe horse trail if 10 Arabian horses are entered to make a purse of $2500. Why do you want to change your proposal now? This doesn't read like your challenge spread far and wide by *THE WESTERN HORSEMAN*. Then you challenged any Arab owner "to an endurance race for money, marbles or chalk." From the words you bloomed in print with, you would let the world believe you are raring to go anyplace for a race with an Arab horse, and you don't care what there is for it, but you want a race.

I am a challenged party and have the right to call the turn on your play in keeping with the condition you named. I can't go to Miles City, Montana, Julesburg, Colo. or someplace else and with that in mind, I have set it right here in California on a suitable location for a good race. I have bet $250 my horse will beat yours. That, likewise is my choice from your challenge, and I have told you that you can put up the same or run without it. My money stays offered to go to the winning horse.

As far as I am concerned, this is race between your horse and mine, called from your challenge and on a first class route for it, over the Sierra Nevada on a horse trail with an Arab horse, and you don't care what there is for it, but you want a race. Auburn to Lake Tahoe. It you want to enlarge the field, that suits me, too, but not with a limit on only one or two breeds of horses. I do not care how many are the entries or what kind of horses. Also I am not interested in raising the ante or entry fee above $250 to keep anybody out. Neither do I have time to monkey with the promotion of entries from others.

If you want to play it open for everybody who may want in, I am for it on the basis they pay their entry to the bank, and the winner take it all. I would like to see anyone else in and welcome. Plenty of good men can be counted on here for starting, finish, trail judges and timers.

You asked if the Auburn-Lake Tahoe horse trail can be followed by an automobile? This is a horse trail and can not be followed by car, although cars can meet the trail and view portions at some scattered points. I will expect you here on any day you select then. Stable accommodations are easily available in Auburn, and I will help any way I can to make this pleasant for you, up to race time.

(s) Wendell Robie.

MILES CITY ENDURANCE RIDE WINNER—Billie Stewart, center, who rode Tim Iron's horse "Drifter" 127 miles from Hell Creek to Miles City in 12 hours, 10 minutes and 15 seconds. Owner Tim Iron of Miles City is shown at the left.

Miles City Endurance Ride Winner—Billie Stewart, center, who rode Tim Iron's horse "Drifter" 127 miles from Hell Creek to Miles City in 12 hours, 10 minutes, and 15 seconds. Owner Tim Iron of Miles City is shown at the left.

Photo by: Charles Barieau

Wendell Robie and his Arabian stallion, Siri, at the finish line of the 1965 Tevis Cup Ride.

Apparently this was the anticlimactic end to the whole affair because later issues of Western Horseman make no further mention of the proposed race. It would sound as though the challenger never arrived and Wendell's beloved Arabian stallion, Bandos, was not able to strut his stuff against Mr. Stewart's Drifter.

It is probable, however, that this original unfulfilled challenge, which Wendell Robie accepted, was the real precipitator for what is now known worldwide as the Tevis Cup Ride or Western States 100 Mile One Day Ride. I have an idea that Mr. Robie was sorely disappointed that the race was never held and so decided to stage a race with some of his good friends. Possibly Mr. Stewart was the force who started modern-day endurance riding by challenging Mr. Robie. Conjecture only, but musing is fun. At any rate, Mr. Robie and four good companions made their initial ride in 1955.

Since that time, thousands of riders have lived Mr. Robie's dream and ridden their good horses on the trail he loved so dearly. In spite of Mother Nature's best efforts to deter it, the Lake Tahoe-Auburn trail continues to cross the Sierra Nevada. It has been burned, flooded, covered with mountains of snow, washed out, scorched by heat and threatened by government bureaucracy. In spite of this, the annual trek by dedicated riders continues each year at the full of the Indian Riding Moon. Wendell had proven repeatedly what he said all along—horses are as good as they ever were. I wonder how many riders measure up to Mr. Robie's standards?

Photo by: Charles Barieau

With the American River below, a rider heads toward Auburn on the
Tevis Cup Trail.

# Chapter Six

## *Pegasus*

*Pegasus — as wild, and as swift,*
*and as buoyant in his flight through the air*
*as any eagle that ever soared into the clouds.*

Nathaniel Hawthorne

The Western States Trail Ride, or Tevis Cup Ride, is not a journey of one day, but rather a year, or maybe even a lifetime. When I send in my entry form months ahead of time, with great certainty, I know my horse and I can win the event. Three months before the anticipated date I lower my sights and think I have a sure chance at Top Ten. A week before ride day, all I want to do is just finish—dead last is even acceptable. The butterflies mount as we arrive at the ride site, and I'll be the happiest person in the world if I can just pass the pre-ride vet examination. At least then I get to start!

I have spent the sleepless nights of the week before figuring out what I need to take with me: food for myself, food for my mount, water buckets, fanny packs, water bottles and on through a hun-

dred other items. Is the truck gassed and oiled? Are the tires in-
flated? Is the extra key where it is supposed to be? Did the horseshoer get the shoes on my horse tightly enough to withstand a
hundred miles of rocks? Are my horse's feet tough enough or
should I have had the farrier pad them?[1] In the excitement, will
my horse be difficult to control at the start of the long journey because I have fed him too much grain or have I shortchanged his
energy demands by not giving him enough? How can I ask my
horse that I've conditioned as a marathon runner in the fog of the
Pacific Coast at sea level to go inland and fight the demands of the
high Sierra for a one hundred mile ultra marathon? Or myself for
that matter, but that is secondary. I have a goal in mind that if
achieved will bring me great satisfaction. My horse does not have
that luxury. He cannot look ahead with anticipation. He will simply follow the orders the years of discipline at the hands of humans have taught him.

I think I have covered every detail a hundred times but the
"what ifs" bounce back and forth in my brain like the sounds of a
galloping horse's hooves upon hard pavement. Soon emotions
take complete control and I wonder why I am putting this kind of
pressure on myself. I ride all the time. This is just another horseback ride. Or is it?

The trip to the ride start site is not restful. As Interstate 80 leads
us from near sea level toward the 10,000-foot peaks, my emotions
take complete control of my life. It is a six-hour trip, the horse
trailer behind a constant reminder of the odyssey I have planned.
We pass Auburn at 1200 feet and I know that it is my target tomorrow. Climbing, climbing, climbing in big undulating curves
on smooth pavement, I gaze to my right and see the towering rock
mountains, the deep canyons and I know my horse won't have
the indulgence of returning to Auburn on the big sweeping turns
and the smooth asphalt that are leading us to the starting line. His
four feet will cover every tortuous twisting rocky steep mountainside by placing one foot inexorably in front of the other. He

must do it in the dark of early dawn, during the long sun beaten hours of the day and then into the dark night once more. Is it fair to make this demand of a horse I profess to love, but don't love enough to say "I am not going to ask you to pit your mortal body against these immortal mountains. God allows me to risk my own body, but did He give me the right to risk yours?" My emotions collide. I can back out, plead ill health, but false bravado prevents it. I want this ride so badly.

When I arrive at the forested camp where the ride will start, all the other horses look more fit, more agile, more vibrant than mine. Have I under trained or has my horse peaked and with too much work been pushed over the edge? I am reminded of a German Equestrian Gold Medal rider who said words that I have not thought of recently but suddenly leap to mind— "When my horse reaches his potential, I do not ask for more. I want to keep him as my friend." I want my horse to still be my friend a hundred miles down the trail. I wonder if anyone else in the world is filled with as much self doubt as I, the unseen burden I carry as I greet fellow riders warmly.

I lead my horse to the veterinarian team. They quiz me as to his recent health history and the amount of training he has had. I sign a statement that says he is free of any performance enhancing drugs. I try to look them straight in the eye so they will know that I am being honest and not trying to cover up something detrimental in my eagerness to be part of the melodrama that seems to unfold each year on ride day. Then one of them listens to his pulse rate and checks his respiration. He assesses his mucous membrane color around the eyeball and pulls back his upper lip. He takes his thumb and presses against my horse's gum to check his capillary refill time. He listens with his stethoscopes for gut sounds to ensure that the digestive system is working properly. He runs a hand over his back to check for sensitivity and then down each leg to check for swelling, cuts or bruises. I scarcely remember to breathe as this professional will determine whether or not my efforts have all been in vain. My horse, however, accepts the inspection calmly, a good sign. The examination continues.

The secretary at the veterinarian's side has my rider card on a clipboard and she faithfully records his observations. As he moves from one area of my horse's body to another without hesitation, I know he has found nothing so far to bar me from my ambitious goal. He picks up my patient animal's legs one by one and flexes the joints, runs his hands down the tendons as he checks for soreness or swelling. He looks at the steel shoe on each foot to be sure they are secure. Finally the moment of truth arrives. I am asked to trot my horse out 120 feet and back again while the veterinarian looks for any gait aberrations, any subtle signs of a limp. If well trained, the horse will trot by my side on a loose lead rope, but most lag back a little. The ground is rough and I cannot really see him as he trots behind me, but if the rope tightens I know he is not showing the forward attitude the veterinarian wants to see. Or does he hurt? As I make the turn to come back toward the vet, I look for any sign in his eyes, a scowl or a frown which means he has seen something he does not like. Does he ask me to repeat the trot out, to circle[2] him to the right or left? Doesn't he know that such a request will make my heart plummet? Or as I head back the longest road in the world, the 120 feet at a vet check, has he a smile and a thumbs-up. If so, I can breathe once again because now I know I will be allowed to start. I exit the vetting area and my friends and family know the verdict from my expression. I will be allowed to start.

Someone comes forward with a large marking crayon and on my horse's hips traces the number that I have been assigned for the next day. At each checkpoint along the trail and each vet stop my number will be recorded. These records show what time I passed a certain area or came into a vet check. If I don't show up, ride management has a good idea of my last recorded location. It also prevents a rider familiar with the trail from taking a shortcut. At the end of the ride, a check will be made to confirm that I passed through all of the checkpoints. If not, I failed to follow the prescribed trail and I will be disqualified.

The Western States Trail is marked every half mile with permanent markers. That may seem adequate to the uninitiated, but to the rider, it is scarcely enough to provide peace of mind. So there is also flagging (bright-colored surveyor's tape) at important junctions. Remember, this is rugged country and missing a turn or straying from the trail can cause a rider to become hopelessly lost in a wilderness area.

A pre-ride meeting held after all the horses are vetted is designed to answer any questions people might have. It frequently raises more doubts than it answers and I just wish it would all be over so I can tend to my horse and prepare for the long wakeful night ahead. I marvel at people who say they rest well the night before the ride. To me, sleep is impossible. My mind is overloaded with a mixture of fear and anticipation.

I return to my trailer where my horse is tied with his hay bag within easy reach. He is munching quietly, so much more at ease than I. Just one last time I want to check all the different items that I will need for my ride tomorrow. I adjust the breast collar that will tighten across my horse's chest as we climb a hill. It will prevent the saddle from slipping backward, which could shift my weight and throw my horse off balance. I brush the saddle pad and carefully inspect it for stickers or rough spots that may irritate my horse's back. I fill my water bottles, pouring a powdered electrolyte mix into one. I place them in the pouches attached to my saddle and make sure the velcro straps that hold them in place are grit free and will adhere tightly to each other. I check the curb strap on the bridle to be certain it will sit properly in the chin groove of my mount, one of the areas where I can apply pressure if needed to slow our forward motion. I grab my hoof pick, lift my horse's legs up one at a time and look for any rocks that may have become lodged in the sole or by the branches of his metal shoes. I try to be casual as I go about my last minute chores, denying the

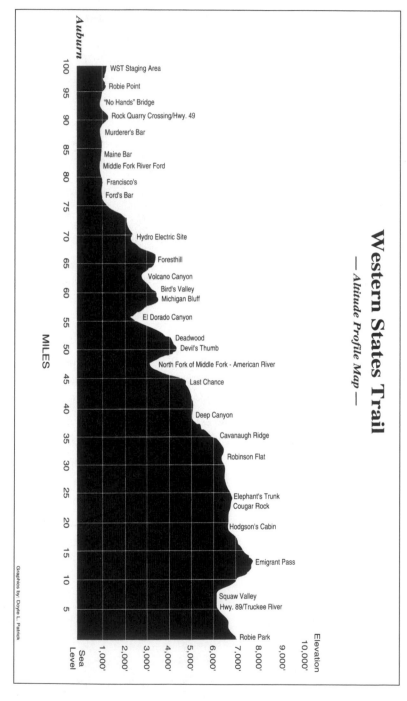

Western States Trail Ride Altitude Profile Map

Western States Trail
— *Altitude Profile Map* —

MILES

Auburn

100
95
90
85
80
75
70
65
60
55
50
45
40
35
30
25
20
15
10
5

WST Staging Area
Robie Point
"No Hands" Bridge
Rock Quarry Crossing/Hwy. 49
Murderer's Bar
Maine Bar
Middle Fork River Ford
Francisco's
Ford's Bar
Hydro Electric Site
Foresthill
Volcano Canyon
Bird's Valley
Michigan Bluff
El Dorado Canyon
Deadwood
Devil's Thumb
North Fork of Middle Fork - American River
Last Chance
Deep Canyon
Cavanaugh Ridge
Robinson Flat
Elephant's Trunk
Cougar Rock
Hodgson's Cabin
Emigrant Pass
Squaw Valley
Hwy. 89/Truckee River
Robie Park

Elevation
10,000'
9,000'
8,000'
7,000'
6,000'
5,000'
4,000'
3,000'
2,000'
1,000'
Sea Level

Graphics by: Doyle L. Patrick

troubling turmoil of self-doubt that is my constant companion. I stop long enough to scratch my horse in the special places that bring him pleasure—behind his ears, between his jaw bones and under his mane at an acupressure point. He lifts his head from the hay bag and stops chewing so he can relish the pleasing sensation. I leave him and climb into the camper to locate the clothes I will wear tomorrow. I find it easier to change into them now than to wait until my 3:30 A.M. rising time when, in the dark and the cold, it will be more difficult. I have always slept the night before in the clothes I will be riding in the next day. I climb into the sleeping bag and set the alarm, a ridiculous move on my part. How many hundreds of time will I glance at it throughout the night as the sleep I crave and need eludes me?

The ride traditionally starts at 5 A.M. I have already been up well over an hour in the dark. I try to eat breakfast, but the butter-flies in the stomach make it difficult. I know I should; I know I need it; I don't want it. But I force it down, add one more Power Bar to my fanny pack, and walk toward my horse. He has been tied to the trailer all night with his feed bag hanging nearby. I note that he has eaten well, but the water bucket is still quite full. I silently wish he had drunk more. Nearby, 250 horses are being saddled and my case of nerves has now transferred to my horse. He senses my anxiety and reacts accordingly by fidgeting and refusing to stand still while I try to place the saddle on his back in the dark. I get the job done and tighten the girth one last time. I ask him to take the bit and I am grateful when he is willing. I put on my helmet, adjust the strap and climb on his back, and, as I do, I get the encouraging words from Bob that have become routine, but that I need so desperately: "I know you will have a good ride."

I have never started a ride unafraid. It is a frenetic time and all I want to do is get going. I question my wisdom at having undertaken this ridiculous event again. Does a silly old woman's craving for adventure dwell in others' hearts as it does in mine or are most better adjusted? Is age driving me in quest of my pioneer roots before I leave my own behind for future generations to seek? Each year I promise my family "just once more." They know I am lying, as do I. But then I see other old-timers' faces in the crowd and I have my answer. I am not alone in my falsehoods. They lie too—to their families, their friends and, as I, to themselves.

I reach the crowded starting line and wait as the seconds pass interminably slowly toward the zero hour—5 A.M. My horse frets, frustrated at the delay, his impatience exceeded only by my own. He lays his ears back and threatens another horse who encroaches upon his space. I jiggle the bit in his mouth to remind him that I am in command and that this is unacceptable behavior. And then the word is given and the lead riders move out with this mass of milling, undulating horseflesh pressing them from the rear. As I pass the starting line I call out my number, and in the confusion I am not sure of it and have to look over my shoulder at the number on my horse's hip to be positive I gave it to the recorder correctly. Ride management then indicates on the ride manifest that I am on the trail.

Two hundred and fifty horses surge in the darkness of a narrow trail. The dust from a thousand horses' hooves is choking. The most hazardous period of the ride is now upon me and it is disheartening. Those with horses out of control will usually pull over and let the main mass go by, sacrificing time in order to preserve the life and limbs of others. Those making the run for the top usually try to start near the front, but pushing the animal too fast in this early stage can leave the rider with a burned-out horse before the finish line is reached. The chess game has started.

My greatest concern is that another horse will crowd mine too closely from behind. If he should step on one of my mount's rear legs or hooves, it can put me out of the race. So I look over my shoulder a few times in hopes that the following rider will get the message: stay back! Accidents arising through the failure of others in the management of their horses is a constant threat. The bank of apprehensive riders and exhilarated horses roils down off the mountain for 7 miles to the road crossing before Squaw Valley.

Already the distance seems long, but my spirits are buoyed by the first streaks of daylight in the morning sky. As I break into the open the horses have already begun to spread out and I hope that my horse is ready to settle down into a smooth aerobic gait that will not drain his energy. I aim for a 7 to 8 mile per hour trot. The excitement of the start is over and as I cross the valley floor, I see an occasional rider pulled over, an obvious sign of a problem. A lame horse? A tied up[3] horse? Or maybe it is just a tack adjustment, changing the length of a stirrup or rearranging a slipped saddle pad. I hope so for, you see, we are all united this day. Young and old, rich and poor bonded by a common goal— Auburn.

Tevis Cup Trail 1987.

The climb under the ski lifts is on a wide but very rocky road. It is daylight now and the gridlock of the first part of the trail is behind me. I try to assess my horse. The good horseman can almost feel intuitively whether his mount is up to the challenge. It escapes me, however, and there is no certainty to bring me inner peace. The 2500-foot climb up the mountain forces my horse to settle down to a good working gait and I begin to see some familiar faces, missed in the dust and darkness of the first few miles. And then suddenly, my nerves quiet, and it all seems worthwhile, the agony of the last weeks replaced by the ecstasy of the moment. At long last, I am on my way.

This is my day, the one for which I have planned and dreamed, the day that I have allowed to assume too much importance in a world filled with issues of real significance. Can I remember to ride my equine partner with my brain as well as the seat of my pants? Our Creator did not design him to go 100 miles in one day. He programmed into him a quick sudden burst of speed to outrun a predator in a short distance. Am I the predator who asks him to do more than what comes naturally to him?

Pacing becomes all-important. His nature makes him want to run to the top. He is as invigorated as I am by chill air and his solidarity with the other horses, where the instinct to travel with the herd may make him try to perform beyond his capabilities. My job is to conserve his strength. I know how many miles we have ahead of us. He does not. I must guard against becoming too involved in conversations with fellow riders. If I am concentrating on what they are saying, I am not focused on what my horse may be trying to tell me. His messages can be subtle. I must not miss them.

The final commitment to the journey ahead is made when I crest the mountains at 8,900 feet and pass the American Flag, reaching for the splendid sky above as it waves atop a stone monument. The last 500 feet follows a rocky jeep road through snow banks left over from a severe Sierra winter. As I reach the top, I get my first glance of the range after range of mountains I must cross this day to achieve my goal. They vary in shades of purple, deep grays and blue, seemingly endless. I fleetingly look back for the last time that day at Squaw Valley and the Lake Tahoe basin I'm leaving behind. I know there is no turning back. Can my sea level horse make the adjustment to altitude that my own lungs tell me must be taxing him? But there is no time for prolonged introspection. I have embarked upon my grinding journey west to the sunburnt hills of my destination, the mighty American River and the night lights of the city of Auburn.

How many hours will I need, and how many footsteps must my pony take? I am allowed 24 hours and, upon occasion, I have needed almost the full time. But on those special days when everything has worked perfectly, I have made the trip in just over 16 hours. What will it be today? Will my companion for the day need my expertise to get him to the finish line? Or will I handicap him because I am not riding up to my ability on this one particular day, a day when I so much want both of us to be at the top of our form?

I jerk my senses back from speculation to the job at hand. The roughest part of the trail is less than a mile away and I know, once there, it will seem interminable. Of necessity, the pace is slowed. I hold my breath and pray that the bogs will not suck my horse's shoes from his feet and that the boulder fields will not lame him. The trail is treacherous and not much more than the width of my horse. There is little room for passing and on this section I am not in charge for it is almost impossible to go by another horse. The boulders are large and, to successfully navigate them, my mount must concentrate on where he will place his feet. How many horses have placed their hooves in the same spots in the century and a half since men first discovered that special ore hidden deep in these mountains? How many horses were sacrificed in man's lust for gold? I must not sacrifice mine today in my lust for Auburn.

The 35-mile checkpoint at Robinson Flat seems far away and I know that many of the horses will be disqualified at the pristine mountain meadow there. A misplaced foot, and my horse will be one of them. The views from the high country are dramatic and

breathtaking but I have little time to reflect on them. My concentration is deep and private as I maneuver my horse around the
rock obstacles on a trail that twists and turns. Or sometimes I release the reins, freeing his head so that he can make his own
choice. It is warmer now and I take off my jacket and tie it around
my waist. I'm thankful that the sun is still at my back. Later in the
day I will have to ride into it and dark glasses and the visor on my
helmet will not be enough to keep me from squinting. I have been
traveling for three hours and my horse is going well. Eager, but
controllable. Perfect! I can take a swig from my water bottle while
I admonish myself for not drinking sooner. Dehydration is the
rider's worst enemy as it is the horse's. Water is scarce on the
backbone of a Sierra mountain ridge.

Dreaded Cougar Rock, the near vertical slippery rock outcrop-
ping whose reputation keeps many from ever attempting this
ride, is approached. It is a mental as well as a physical challenge.
Watching the horses that precede us stretch and strain to find a
foothold stretches and strains my confidence as well. Then my
horse's steel-shod hooves, governed by this remarkable animal I
am aboard, start the ascent which must carry us both over this
hurdle. I try to keep my weight centered properly as he alternate-
ly pulls and lunges. With previously untapped vigor, he makes
one last effort and we are propelled over the top. We leave Cougar
Rock behind and I sigh audibly.

As I approach Red Star Ridge, I know that volunteers and a veterinarian will be there in case of need, kind souls who will hand
me paper cups filled with water and offer to hold my horse if I
need a pit stop. They are the real heroes of our sport. After their
greatly appreciated attention, I am refreshed and life suddenly
gets easier. I look at my watch and estimate my time of arrival at
the first veterinarian hold point. The seven miles of lumber road
leading to the next stop, Robinson Flat, can be done at a good trot
and my horse welcomes the relief of this dusty road from the
miles of narrow rocky trails. If he is sound,[4] I know we have tri-

umphed over those unforgiving boulder fields we have just so laboriously traversed. Arrival at Robinson Flat means the first third of the ride is behind me. It has taken me six hours—six hours of draining the stored energy of my horse as well as my own. We will have one hour to try to replenish it.

Robinson Flat is a madhouse. How could I have thought of it as a pristine meadow? Vehicles, horses, hundreds of people. My eyes seek the special person that I know is going to help me for the next hour. Bob will have spent three to four hours driving to reach this spot. He will have been stopped a mile before his destination to avoid clogging access roads and must wait for the shuttle truck to carry him the last mile with the things so vital to my horse and me. A bag full of hay, water buckets and my food will all be laid out so that my horse and I can make the most of the one-hour hold.

I jump from my horse as Bob greets us and leads us in the last one-hundred yards, past the timer who records my number and my arrival time, past the questioning onlookers who call out to see if I have seen the rider for whom they are waiting. It is probably around 11 A.M. Bob unsaddles my horse. From the moment I timed in, I am allowed 30 minutes in which to present my horse to the veterinarians for inspection. If I think his pulse and respiration rates are within the allowable parameters, I will go directly to the vet checking area. If not, I will take him to the spot Bob has picked out. While he cools and relaxes, my eyes fixate on my watch. Every minute lost waiting for his pulse to drop, is a minute less of forward motion. But he seems at ease and comfortable. I head to the examination area and on the way, I water him and feed him a few handfuls of hay to get his gut sounds going. I watch his sides to observe how fast he is breathing and I press a stethoscope against his chest cavity. If I was playing it smart, I slowed my pace the last mile into Robinson Flat so that his recovery from heavy exertion will have already started before I arrive. His heart rate must be at 60 or fewer beats per minute. When he reaches that point, I lead him to the veterinarian examining area.

Somehow I have calmed down and realize that if my horse does not pass this vet check, the earth will continue to turn and the sun will rise tomorrow. The more fortunate will continue down the trail without us. We have survived the start and the roughest part of the trail. If we get no farther, it has been worth the time, effort and mental agony I have put myself through to reach this point. I dared to risk failure and that alone is all I need. I am a realist. I know that only about half of those calling their numbers out at the beginning of the ride early this morning will make it to Auburn where their numbers will be recorded for the last time as they cross the finish line. Of the half that fail, a third of them will be eliminated at this first veterinarian checkpoint. Will I be one of them? I have no reason to think so. My horse has been going well, but. . . .

The scene from the night before is repeated and once again I search the veterinarian's face to know the verdict. He gives letter grades on my horse's "report" card. A quick rundown—I want to see A's and B's. C's are reason for concern. A "D" will probably result in disqualification. The check is thorough, but takes only several minutes. WE pass. The report card that I must carry with me at all times is returned to me and I tuck it carefully into my fanny pack. We, this wonderful horse and I, will be allowed back on the trail.

Bob leads us to the spot he has picked out for our short respite—hay for my horse, food for me and water for us both. We now have less than an hour to rest and eat. It is important that my horse take care of his needs. He has come 35 miles and he requires fuel to keep his great body moving down the trail. His carefully prepared grain ration is measured and liberally sprinkled with carrots and apples. Salt is administered if he is drinking well, but not otherwise. I monitor his intake and feel gratified as he eats and drinks. His grey coat, that I so meticulously groomed last night, is covered with the red dust of the trail, the same dust that most likely encased the bodies of his forebearers carrying the gold out of "them thar hills." My horse has his roots just as I have mine. Perhaps his are buried here too.

Bob washes the four legs that have carried me so far already this morning. Then he sponges the dried sweat from my horse's back, neck and sides. He checks to see that there are no loose shoes, then refills my water bottles and takes the jacket from my waist. I am ready to continue. The heat has started to build and as I leave, Bob drapes a wet towel around my neck and dashes my horse with water. We will soon dry, my horse and I, but it will help us for a short while. The timer duly records our departure and we are on our way on the second leg of our journey.

Leaving the vet check, we quickly plunge into the isolation of a forest trail. The roughest part of the trail is behind us, but the toughest part is our next section. There is a difference. The riders are farther apart now and there may be long minutes when my horse and I are by ourselves and a marvelous stillness envelops us, broken only by the sounds of his hooves hitting the rocks that never end. I talk to my horse. It is not much of a discourse. They are words of encouragement or praise for him when a hill is topped, a stream crossed, a frightening object successfully passed. A pat or rub on the neck lets him know that I am his partner in this day's adventure and that we are working in concert. In the same way, a sharper edge to my voice when he crowds another horse or fails to respond to a signal, tells him that I am displeased. Languor is not for us this day. We must keep moving, inexorably west.

If I prefer company, a brief pause and others will come along. Or, if I set my pace a bit faster, I am likely to overtake other contestants and I can decide to pass them or choose to stay with the group. My decision will depend on several things. Knowing my horse is of the utmost significance here because it is his preference, not mine, that is important. My wonderful Gazal, that carried me so successfully down this trail for seven consecutive years, could not stand to be alone. He simply liked company of his own kind and if isolated from them, would whinny and go down the trail with his equine brakes on, stiff-legged and with a defeated air. If he caught sight of horses ahead, his attitude change was remarkable. Or if he sensed horses coming from the rear, he would stop and listen and wait for them to catch up. He is telling me that God programmed him to be a herd animal and that is what he is going to be. So with Gazal I always preferred to ride with others. But, when I did this, I lost the yardstick by which I should be judging my horse. A tired horse finds security in numbers and can be sucked along by a group of his own kind beyond his abilities. His valiant effort to keep up with those more fit than himself can be his and, in turn, my undoing if he fails to recover at the next veterinarian check point. Occasionally I have ridden horses who perform better by themselves. *Marinera, the most competitive of horses I have ridden, was the prime example. She needed the herd only if she could be in front. Alone, she was perfection and I could rate her and "ride my own ride." In a crowd she wasted energy she could not afford in her efforts to maintain the lead.

The relationship between a rider and his horse trying to perform at the highest level is extremely complex. Is this an animal so generous of his own body that he will give until he drops from exhaustion? Or is his desire to please less bold and he will govern his own limits of exertion? The outcome of the ride and the horse's welfare depend on the rider's ability to judge and ride the horse accordingly.

As I continue down the trail, I mull over the gossip from Robinson Flat. Word spreads quickly as to who was disqualified and found the end of the trail too soon. I know who the front runners are and my general position in the pack. I know that about 30 of the starters did not make it past Robinson Flat. Most of them found that stone out there with their name on it, the one that dashes dreams when one misplaced hoof comes down too hard. A few will not have shown the metabolic recovery the veterinarian wanted—perhaps a pulse that would not drop or a lack of gut sounds or a serious case of dehydration that results in disqualification.

Rocky Cavanaugh Ridge leads me farther west until I hit the hard gravel road that descends to Deep Canyon and the ice-cold stream, the first water since leaving Robinson Flat. It is just past midday and the sun is at its zenith. Our five A.M. start seems distant, such a very long time ago. I stand my horse in the water. In the morning, before leaving, I tied a cord to a sponge and hooked it on my saddle. From the back of my horse, I drop it into the cool waters and squeeze it over his neck and shoulders and then down my own back. I wash my face with the same sponge and then, with reluctance, signal with a light pull on the reins, that we still have trail to cover. He is refreshed and we hurry up the hill to Dusty Corners. I make the turn to the right. I'm now out from under the protection of the forest and the shadows of the branches that helped fight the heat. There is no sweat on my horse. It is hot, but the humidity is low and any sweat quickly evaporates in the dry air in an effort to keep 900 pounds of horseflesh cool. Totally exposed under the cloudless sky, with an unmerciful sun above, my horse carries me toward Last Chance and the formidable canyons that lie beyond.

When the forest road gives way to the narrow hairpin turns and twisting contortions of the route to the bottom of the menacing canyon, I know I must descend 1600 feet in the next few miles. Many riders jump off at this point and run down the trail with their horse running behind them. This relieves the horse of the weight of the rider and the pressure on his shoulders and front legs that the jolting ride to the bottom can produce. It also gives a fit rider a chance to stretch his own limbs that frequently cry for mercy after hours in the saddle. A riderless horse led by a good runner can navigate the route to the bottom much faster than a mounted rider. On the uphill many riders "tail."[5] I do not favor my horse with these luxuries. The trail is too rough and my aged ankles too given to twisting to risk it.

At the bottom I have a choice. I can go into the river to make the crossing or I can choose the swinging bridge to get to the other side. If I pick the water route, I must maneuver my horse over the slippery boulders on the river's edge and cross the river where the footing is hazardous. There are advantages to this choice, though. The belly-deep cooling water can revive a horse. The temperature, well over the 100-degree mark now, is a major factor affecting our performance. My other choice is to cross the swinging bridge over the Middle Fork of the North Fork of the American River. It is only one horse wide and perhaps sixty feet long. Anchored securely at both ends, it will support the weight of several horses and riders at a time, but this creates another hazard. At about midpoint it starts to sway and swing. Past experiences tell me that this is a sensation horses do not relish anymore than the riders on their backs. I choose the bridge this day instead of the river crossing. My horse is a flight animal by nature and I can feel his hesitation as he places one forefoot upon the shaky surface. He responds to my heels in his side, but midway he starts to rush. The distance is short and once on the ground he quickly settles down. Some horses refuse the bridge, but most will follow a rider who tries to lead them across. I do not have this much courage. When the bridge starts to sway, I know a panicked horse can go only one way and I don't want to be trampled. Four or five hundred feet up the trail, if it has been a wet winter, there will be a small pool of water where my horse can sip as much as he wants. I prefer this to the risky river crossing, but I have had horses totally refuse the bridge and have had to retrace my steps back to the river and ford it through the slippery rocks.

The 1600-foot climb out of the canyon, past the huge landmark rock called Devil's Thumb, is slow and arduous. I am too hot, too thirsty and too tired. Why am I doing this? Tacking back and forth, the trail is frighteningly narrow and there are very few places where I can pass, or pull over to let another horse pass me. Riders try to be courteous, but the hours have taken their toll, the heat has sapped the energy of man and beast and the journey to the top seems to take forever. Even the shade of the trees offers no relief from the heat, nor does a wayward breeze heroically find its way to us. I look skyward hoping to catch a glimpse of the top of the ridge, but I have not come far enough. I do not know how many switchbacks there are. Somebody must have counted them in the past. Why haven't I? Then I could tick them off one by one and know that I am making progress. At the moment, I feel there is no end to them.

Then, to my tremendous relief, I see sky ahead of me instead of mountainside, and I know that the first of the three great canyons has been mastered by my horse. The trail levels and volunteers standing near the water trough make life worth living again for this team my horse and I have become. They point us toward the Deadwood vet check just three miles further down the ridge top. My horse willingly assumes an easy going trot and the doldrums that pursued us relentlessly on the canyon climb vanish. The access to the remote and rugged Deadwood area is difficult so personal crews are not allowed, but dedicated ride volunteers are assigned to help the riders. I am offered fresh cantaloupe, water-melon and every imaginable cold drink. And now it is time once more to present my horse to the veterinarians. We are about 56 miles into our journey, past the halfway mark, and that knowl-edge alone buoys my spirit.

The veterinarians are especially cautious with this examina-tion. They are not looking at fresh horses anymore, but tiring ones. In the next seven miles they know we will descend 2500 feet into El Dorado Canyon and then have to climb nearly 2000 feet out of it. As with the first daunting canyon, there will be no breeze and the walls of this mighty scar on the earth's surface will be hot to the touch. The heat is trapped and it does not move—stifling, unceasing. A horse in trouble can only come out under his own power and so they must be certain the animal can safely maneuver through this section. This is not a mandatory hold, but rather a checkpoint where my mount and I can continue as soon as he meets the criteria of not more than 60 heart beats per minute and shows at the trot-out that he remains sound. I can loiter here, but time lost cannot be regained, so I push on, and with each step reduce by one the thousands my horse must still take. I once more look a canyon in the face and know I have to conquer it.

I start the descent. God, it's hot. Will I ever be cool again? But my horse feels strong and is obviously handling the day with less discouragement than I. If I can just get to the Michigan Bluff vet stop I will see Bob.[6] My horse and I will have an hour to rest and gain back the strength that has been sapped from both of our bodies. It is a seven-mile journey from Deadwood to Michigan Bluff— the seven longest miles of the day.

Cresting a ridge once more and arriving in the late afternoon, I enter this Gold Rush town to a flurry of activity. Its one narrow street allows no room to spread out and the horses that have made it this far are of necessity crowded too closely together. What they need most is a restful spot to refuel once more and perhaps catch a short nap. The few trees in town offer only partial shade for those who get there first and the bustling activity allows little rest.

The worst of the trail, the high country, the boulder fields, the two most formidable deep canyons, are behind us. The worst of the 17,000 feet of ascent and 22,000 feet of descent I am asking my horse to do this day has been surmounted by his sure-footedness. But the vet check is thorough here; these horses have gone 63 miles. Only the most fit will leave under their own power, the others by horse trailers with their disappointed riders at their sides. I watch once more as the veterinarian checks my horse's pulse and respiration parameters, and as he runs his hands over his body and listens with his stethoscope to that wonderful heart beating inside this treasured animal. And then I start my trot out on the one paved street in the town. I do not need to look back at my horse to see if he is trotting soundly. I can hear the cadence of his hooves on the pavement; the rhythm is perfect and I know all is well.

Dreams have been lost this day for many of the riders, but

many still search for fulfillment and I am one of the fortunate ones. The crowd claps as I leave. They do this for all the riders for they know how far they have come and that encroaching darkness now becomes the common enemy. The blistering sun I despised all day has become my friend and I do not want it to leave the western sky. I want to see where I am going, but I know, that when night settles, it will soon be impossible and I must depend on my horse's far more acute eyesight to lead us safely. It is probably the only place in the ride where I urge my horse beyond what he wants to give me. I squeeze him with my legs and at the same time I rub his neck to encourage him.

The lengthening shadows tell me I must pick up the pace because soon it will be slowed by the revolution of the earth as one more day enters its final stretch. Experience has taught me that early dusk usually finds the horses at their lowest ebb. As the heat of the day subsides, I know that my companion that seemed so weary leaving Michigan Bluff will sense that his journey is in the last stages. We have come 63 miles—just 37 to go. Just?

We hurry through the town of Foresthill and my horse unexpectedly jumps sideways at the sight of a plastic bag on the ground. My feet slip from the stirrups and I start to slide from the saddle. Miraculously, I somehow regain my balance and my feet struggle to find the flopping stirrups as my horse continues trotting, now faster. His shying at the bag helped to break his boredom and he is feeling a bit cocky that he caught me by surprise. But how happy I am. An exhausted horse does not react with such suddenness. My horse has just told me that he is feeling well and I do not have to chastise myself for urging him to a faster pace earlier. The townspeople line the one main street to watch the riders go by. I spot some leaning against a pickup truck with cold, wonderful thirst-quenching beers in their hands. I call out: "Want to trade places?" There is laughter but no takers. But then, I didn't mean it anyway. There is no one I would trade places with this day.

The sounds of civilization fade as I leave Foresthill and descend to the California Loop. The trail hangs precariously on the side of a canyon wall and dusk, conspiring against me, robs me of the view of the American River a thousand feet below. It is 13 miles to Francisco's and the next checkpoint. Thirteen. I am glad that I am not superstitious. Or am I? Once again there are many switch backs and in the darkness I hope my horse sees them because I cannot. An occasional glance through the shifting shadows produces a familiar spot to restore my fading confidence. It is not a place where I want him to step off the trail. Memories of previous rides tell me that it helps to tuck in behind someone on a white or grey horse, since a black or brown horse is practically invisible even though he may be only a few feet ahead. This is the period when I have to trust my horse completely; a misstep could result in disaster for us both. I know he is tired, but I also know his self-preservation instinct is strong. And, his eyesight is far keener than mine in the dark. The riders now tend to bunch up. There is some talk, but much of it is nervous chatter meant to keep spirits high. I seem to mostly listen, pensively lost in my own thoughts more than those of my fellow riders. I have heard that some people say they almost go to sleep on their horses. I cannot believe it. I am 16 hours into this ride with only two one-hour rest periods and two other brief stops. My mind fails to give me surcease from the thoughts that crowd it and I long to get off the mountain and down to the river which will lead me to Auburn.

Francisco's is not easily found by day or night. I try to see the time on my watch in the darkness, but to no avail. I am jammed up behind a group of slow riders and am frustrated that I cannot pass on the narrow trail. I can tell my horse would need no inducement to step out more briskly. But I am lenient with my fellow riders, some of them making their first effort to put the final legs of this 100 mile trail into their past and a silver buckle on their belts.

It is hard to fathom that we have not reached Francisco's yet. It must be nearly three hours since we left the outskirts of Foresthill. Discouragement is a subtle master. It does not sweep you into one grand embrace, but sneaks up in little increments. It toys with you

| | | | FROM | TO | CHECK | | Cut-Off |
|---|---|---|---|---|---|---|---|
| FROM | TO | MILEAGE | ROBIE | AUBURN | TYPE | P&R | Time |
| Robie Park | SV High Camp | 9.8 | 9.8 | 90.2 | Water + Vet Available | | |
| Squaw Vally Gate | Lyon Ridge | 11.6 | 21.4 | 78.6 | Trot-By (Vet Available) | | |
| Lyon Ridge | Red Star Ridge | 7.0 | 28.4 | 71.6 | Water Only ~ NO CREWS | | |
| Red Star Ridge | Robinson Flat | 7.4 | 35.8 | 64.2 | 60 min (Gate* to Hold) | 60/48 | 12:45pm |
| Robinson Flat | Dusty Corners | 10.4 | 46.2 | 53.8 | Trot-By/Spot Check | SOUND | 0 |
| Dusty Corners | Pacific Slab Mine | 3.4 | 49.6 | 50.4 | Trot By/Spot Check | | |
| Pacific Slab Mine | Devil's Thumb | 4.7 | 54.3 | 45.7 | Water Only ~ NO CREWS | | |
| Devil's Thumb | Deadwood | 1.9 | 56.2 | 43.8 | Gate* ~ NO CREWS | 68/48 | 5:45pm |
| Deadwood | El Dorado Creek | 3.5 | 59.7 | 40.3 | (info only) | | |
| El Dorado Creek | Michigan Bluff | 2.9 | 62.6 | 37.4 | 15 min (Gate* to Hold) | 64/48 | 7:15pm |
| Michigan Bluff | Foresthill | 6.1 | 68.7 | 31.3 | 60 min (Gate* to Hold) | 68/48 | 8:45pm |
| Foresthill | CA #2 | 9.7 | 78.4 | 21.6 | (info only) NO CREWS | | |
| CA #2 | Francisco's | 7.7 | 86.1 | 13.9 | Gate* ~ NO CREWS | 68/48 | 1:45am |
| Francisco's | River Xing | 3.4 | 89.5 | 10.5 | (info only) | | |
| River Xing | Lower Quarry | 4.9 | 94.4 | 5.6 | Gate* ~ NO CREWS | 68/48 | 4:15am** |
| Lower Quarry | No Hands Bridge | 1.2 | 95.6 | 4.4 | (info only) | | |
| No Hands Bridge | Overlook Finish | 4.3 | 99.9 | 0.1 | Meet Criteria/Finish | | 5:15am |
| Overlook Finish | McCann Stadium | 0.1 | 100.0 | | 1 Hr Re-check*** | TBD | |

**Western States Trail Ride-Tevis Cup 100 Miles One Day - July 15, 2000**
CHECKPOINT INFORMATION
Ride starts 5:15am - All riders must leave park by 5:30am

*Gate=when criteria reached, present horse. Only one 15 min recheck if criteria not met initially. P & R subject to change
**Time rider MUST leave this checkpoint.     ***Must pass vet evaluation for metabolic status/soundness.
HAGGIN CUP EXAMS HELD ON SUNDAY AT 10:00 AM ~ ALL FIRST TEN QUALIFIED HORSES SHOULD BE PRESENTED (Don't leave GCFG)

Checkpoint Information from 2000 Participant Guide.

until you cannot escape and so I fight it desperately because I know my horse will sense my loss of purpose and then he, too, will lose heart. I want to relax, to sag in my saddle, but once again, my horse's needs are primary. A well balanced rider takes less toll on a mount's body and it is his body that must get us to Auburn. We need a respite and Francisco's continues to elude us. Did we miss the trail, take a wrong turn? Uncertainty and self doubt wash over me and my toughest fight now is to stay up-beat, optimistic and to somehow transmit these feelings to my horse. But he does not flag. It is he who lifts my spirits; my admiration and respect for his gallantry is boundless.

I no longer crave the sounds of summer, the crickets joyous chorus. I want the frenzied tension of a vet stop, the ever hovering question and suspense of "will I be allowed to continue?" I hear a hum in the distance and with each forward step it becomes louder. I smile in the darkness where no one can see my sudden shift in moods. The generator's noisy motor means Francisco's is within calling distance. What a glorious sound! Around a corner and the floodlit veterinarian area lights the faces of the horses and riders that have preceded me to this stop. I can read the posture of both and instinctively know which have found more miles unconquerable this day.

Once again volunteers rush to the riders as we emerge from the blackness. They lead us to water and question us about our personal needs. Do I want a sandwich, a cold drink? Yes, I do, but my horse must come first. Only when he has passed the vet check and is replenishing his own needs can I think about my own. Can they bring my horse some hay? They do and then once more a veterinarian confirms that I am one of the lucky ones today. I can continue. I turn to a selfless volunteer and take from her hands the sandwich and iced tea offered me earlier. She and the others are angels without wings—angels with dirt and grime on their faces who are staying up all night to help a stranger achieve a goal. No rewarding silver belt buckles for them at the Award Banquet tomorrow. They must settle for the "thank you" from tired riders who sometimes forget.

As with the vet check at Deadwood, I am free to leave once the veterinarians say that I can continue. But I loiter and I see in the faces of friends and strangers the verdict they have been handed. The veterinarians are on the riders' side and are reluctant to disqualify anyone at this point since they know how far they have come. They also know that the trailer ride for the disqualified horses out of Francisco's to White Oaks Flat is long and difficult. It is only 14 miles by trail of comparatively easy going to the finish. They want us to get there. I am anxious to leave. But my horse's head is buried deep in the rich alfalfa hay and he is eating ravenously. I allow him the luxury but briefly, for we still have trail ahead of us. He accepts the bit without hesitation and we leave the floodlit area and plunge into the darkness once more. I now welcome the fading hum of the generator and the return to the sounds of summer, a total reversal of my feelings but a short time ago. I ask for more miles from this horse that has already given me so many this day and his silent acquiescence brings us closer to our goal with each step. Not all of those with whom I rode into Francisco's have returned to the trail with me. For some it was the end of the line and the long, hard trailer ride back to camp.

Silence engulfs us. The moon is up now, but it is not the guiding light it should be. I'm in a deep canyon with many trees and the moon has to struggle to find me. It casts strange shadows and the boulders by the side of the trail look more like giant holes in the ground. I have to resist the impulse to guide my horse around them. He knows so much more than I do. My night vision is poor and my depth perception in the dark on a moving horse very faulty. I feel as though I am sitting on something much taller than my five foot high horse. I wonder how his legs can be long enough to reach the ground, but also realize I am fortunate to have never experienced the vertigo that bothers so many riders in the dark.

I reach forward and rub my horse's neck and tell him he is a good boy and that we are almost there. But I don't have to tell him because he knows. He senses my optimism and responds with renewed energy. He is holding his head higher and he has quickened his step.

We finally descend to the American River, and the sandy beach leads us to the river crossing. Glow sticks have been placed in the water to guide the riders across to the other side where more volunteers have built a bonfire. Why, I can remember the days when I just crossed in the dark and kept my fingers crossed that I'd find a landing on the other side. No guides, no glow sticks. But then, who wants old-timers to tell about how much tougher it "used to be?" The water can be belly deep and a short horse may even have to swim a bit. My boots fill with water and it feels so delicious. The harsh burning sensation caused by the friction of my feet in the stirrups all day is suddenly gone and I am refreshed. My horse thrusts his nose and mouth into the current and sucks deeply. We emerge on the other side ready and eager for the home stretch. The going is good now for almost the first time this long day. The dirt road is wide with few obstacles to trip an unsuspecting horse in the dark. We are flying now—the two of us—and my spirits soar with each lengthening ground covering stride. The road bends and I see the lights of Auburn ahead. I have come about 92 miles and I reflect on why they can't build a trail that will just take us straight on into those flickering city lights. But darkness returns with the next turn we make and I tritely tell myself not to count my chickens before they are hatched. We are not there yet, but oh my, I am deliriously happy. Is it possible to want something to end while wishing it will go on forever?

Floodlamps bathe the lower rock quarry outside of Auburn and, for almost the last time, I will present my horse to the veterinarians and pray they will tell me to "go on in." They do! There is no mandatory hold time here, but once more I linger awhile so my hungry horse can eat. How can I deny him? Each minute we stay means a lower placing at the finish line as other horses pull out onto the home stretch while I let my horse satisfy his hunger. But I am more than happy to relinquish a few places so he can have the smallest of rewards for all he has given me this day. Finally I raise his head and mount him for the last stretch of trail. Next to me a stranger rides, a young man generations removed from me in age. We glance at each other and, as our eyes meet in the fading light of the vet stop, we spontaneously "high five" each other. We both know that victory is only 6 miles ahead of us, not 100, not 50—just 6! Buoyed by that knowledge, he pulls ahead of me into the darkness and my horse and I continue on alone. We cross Highway 49, blinded somewhat by the headlights of on-coming cars that have been stopped by crossing guards to let us pass. Then one last horrible, but thankfully short, stretch of treacherous trail brings us to "No Hands Bridge." An old abandoned railroad trestle, it stands 80 feet over the riverbed and for the first time this day, there is nothing to my right or left except space.[7] I think of two departed friends who loved this trail so much their ashes were scattered from this bridge from the backs of the running horses they left behind. My gaze plunges and the moonlight reflecting on the American River takes my breath away and I want this moment frozen in time. The water flows over the rocks like smooth silk and the graceful bends of the river mesmerize me. Has there ever been a more beautiful sight?

I now have four miles to go to complete my journey. My horse trots along eagerly with a loose rein on the old railroad right-of-way that winds above the river. The path abruptly stops and we dip sharply down into what has been nicknamed 'The Black Hole of Calcutta.' How had I forgotten about this one last awful hazard, this terrible place of darkness? No moonlight penetrates its depths. In the awful blackness I am slapped in the face by an overhanging branch. I feel my horse's feet search for security in the rocky creek bed, but they slip off the stones and for the first time today he seems hesitant and unsure of himself. He has been the confident one this day, not I. I silently plead with him not to fail me now. He hears the trickling water, feels it about his ankles and dips his head to take a well earned drink. In the blackness I feel a surge of panic and I pull his head up, denying him his right. Stridently I say, "Please horse, get me out of here." He senses my urgency and, scrambling, returns to the solid ground of the old railroad bed, now bathed in moonlight. Tension is transcended by an almost surreal serenity as we leave the obscureness of the 'Black Hole' behind us. The finish line is only a couple of miles down this road. The mountain ranges have been surmounted, the rivers crossed, our hoof prints embedded on the steep trails. We have triumphed. Happiness fades briefly to wistfulness the last few miles. I savor them for the last time and wish the ride were longer. I do not want this day to end.

Out of the darkness we come into the lights and I see the finish line official. I call out my number for the final time. I do not have to look at my horse's hip this time to confirm it. Together we have beaten the trail and the clock, this wonderful animal and I. We head for the water trough that my horse seeks—the cool liquid that I had guiltily withheld from him back on the trail. I search for Bob in the crowd and he is there. I look at him and our eyes meet

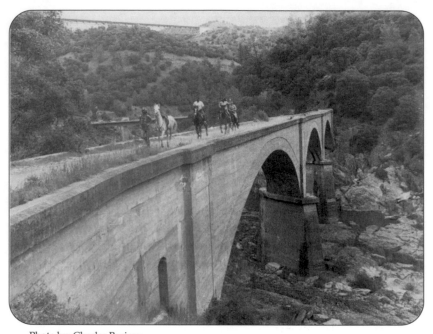

Photo by: Charles Barieau
No Hands Bridge—1964.

and I tell him "I had a good ride. You said I would." I have found bliss, my moment of exultation.

The finish line veterinarian tells me I can proceed to the Gold County Fairground's Stadium, the ceremonial finish a block away. I bring my horse onto the track and I nudge his soft flanks just one more time. He breaks into a canter, and we cross the last few hundred feet of a hundred mile ride running. I jump off and wrap my arms around his neck as his sweet breath warms my cheek. I bury my face in the silky mane and the tears flow as they did in my childhood, not because the world has been unjust, but because it has been so very right. I had my Pegasus today. Together we reached the stars.

# CHAPTER SEVEN

# Lo and Behold and *Marinera

*Of all God's creatures, none can compare
to the horse.*

Leonardo da Vinci

When I first heard of the Tevis Cup Ride, my goal in life seemed to be its successful completion—just once, and I could live happily ever after. My aspirations went no further, or so I thought. It was only a short time after the ride that I began to think of reasons why I should tackle that trail again. I felt that I had "lucked" through the ride on a seasoned endurance horse with a strong homing instinct. It didn't seem as though the personal triumph was as great as if I had started a horse from scratch. My own horse, Lady Kay, my original choice, had proved unsuitable for this type of an endeavor. Chagatai, with his look of eagles intact, had been returned to Dru and his Auburn home. That should have been the end of it. But it was not, nor is it 37 years later. It was 1965, and, as far as I know, I was the only person in the Santa Clara Valley who had even the least interest in this type of riding or who

73

had even heard the term "endurance riding." There was no one to talk with concerning my passion and my friends dismissed the subject politely with an "Oh, it sounds like fun" and changed the subject. I dwelled on it daily. My parents said they were proud of my accomplishment, but I knew that they had little comprehension of the personal impact the Tevis Cup Ride can deal some people, including their daughter.

With three teenagers and a husband dedicated to his business and community activities, it seemed selfish to think of purchasing another horse. It was now 1966, and "THE" ride was in only six months. Its beckoning call was loud and clear. My salvation came while reading a copy of *Western Horseman.* There was an article about a new breed of horse being introduced into the country, primarily by a man named Verne Albright. The article said that Mr. Albright lived in Los Gatos, fortuitously only a few miles from my Saratoga home. He discussed a particular breed, the Peruvian Paso, renowned in Peru for its endurance. The word "paso," in popular usage, refers to the unique gait of this South American breed. Most breeds of horses are diagonally gaited with the front foot on one side hitting the ground at the same time as the rear foot on the opposite side. This is not particularly comfortable and undoubtedly the basis for the popular notion that if you ride for very long, you have to eat your dinner off the mantelpiece. Most who ride frequently know how to soften the pounding by posting (rising to the trot) or learning to sit the trot by absorbing the shock in other parts of the body, mainly the knee, hip and ankle joints. The Peruvian Paso horse is born with a different footfall pattern which places the rear foot on one side down while the front foot on the same side hits the ground a split second later. Then the two on the other side of the body follow the same pattern. There is also an outward thrust of the forelegs unique to the breed and which I believe contributes to their sure-footedness. My Peruvian horses don't seem to ever stumble and I attribute it to their action of lifting the foot outward and higher rather than dragging it forward in a straighter path as other breeds do. It is also true that the gait has no aerial phase (one foot is always on the ground) so the horse's entire weight does not return to the earth in an "unfamiliar" location. The ride is remarkably smooth and most Peruvian horse shows in America have a class where the riders hold glasses of champagne while circling the arena at ever-increasing speeds until the one with the fullest glass of champagne at the end wins the prize.

Smooth riding horses were introduced into Peru in the 16th century by Pizzaro, who brought a handful of gaited horses from Spain. They were the result of popular breeding practices of those times, taking the smoothest stallions, breeding them to the smoothest mares, and gradually refining the process until the desired gait was achieved. Popular types used for breeding were the Barb, the Andalusian and the Spanish Jennet, which was known for a smooth ambling gait. In the 1960s these fluid-riding horses from Peru were just beginning to be imported into the United States.

Verne, one of the breed's earliest and most dedicated fanciers, made several buying trips to Peru on behalf of clients wanting to import these special horses to this country. With great presumption, I called Mr. Albright and told him I thought he should loan me one of these remarkable animals so that I could prove his claim that they had great endurance by riding one through the 100-Mile Tevis Cup Ride. He pondered my request, checked with a client and brought into my life a 6-year-old Peruvian mare by the name of "*Marinera."[1] No, not the spaghetti sauce (spelled and pronounced differently), but rather she was named after a dance they do in Peru. *Marinera (the Mar is pronounced Mar, not mare) was strong, full of desire and, in spirit, still a wild, frightened horse. She tolerated me upon her back out of fear of the consequences if she did not. Her early Peruvian training had taught her obedience at the hands of man and it is a wonder she survived my incessant demands. She never walked a step in her life but pasoed or cantered swiftly from one side of the Santa Cruz Mountains, where she was boarded, to the other and I thrilled to every step. She was my dream horse, the horse of my childhood fantasies.

In those days, the popular opinion was that you couldn't hurt a horse and we had grown up hearing phrases such as "tough as a horse" or how someone "ate like a horse." *Marinera stayed sound and I wonder how, for there was no place to go for information on this type of long distance riding. And I was very ignorant—a good rider, but not a good horsewoman, and there is a vast difference. A good rider has balance, coordination and a sense of timing. He finds the horse's center of gravity and stays in rhythm with the motion of the horse. These are more or less inborn talents or learned through long hours in the saddle. But a good rider is not necessarily a good horseman. The latter has spent untold hours listening, reading, observing and gaining hands-on experience with many horses. In most cases, it takes more than one horse to develop a good horseman. In the days when the horse was the difference between life and death of a rider, lessons were quickly learned. The horse's welfare was paramount for survival and his needs came first. Great attention was given to feeding and foot care. Riders learned how to assess their horse's well being by observation and sometimes recognizing very subtle signs that all was not well. The horse that was not eating well, or that lay down for long periods, or whose eyes were dull had a problem. The savvy horseman made corrections before the situation deteriorated.

I know that most people are brought up to believe that the horse is a very tough animal. I was. I think it is a mistaken assumption. The domesticated horse is extremely fragile. In the wild, his natural state, he roams miles each day, filling his stomach frequently with small amounts of nourishment. In a captive environment, he is usually fed large amounts twice a day and the resulting digestive disturbances keep many a veterinarian in practice. Ulcers are common place and colic is frequent. A horse that gets into a grain barrel when no one is looking is most likely going to be in serious trouble and very possibly die. He can not regurgitate and he is unable to cope with the overload to his sensitive digestive processes. Being confined in small areas denies him the exercise he needs for general well-being. The healthy hoof requires exercise to keep the blood pumping through it and promote normal growth. The confined horse's feet suffer from too little movement and most lameness can be attributed to the fact that the animal is not leading the life which nature intended. The good horseman attempts to "read" his horse and approximate his natural state as closely as possible. And, hopefully, the well-being of the horse is a priority and he treats the animal with compassion, forming a partnership.

When I started endurance riding, there was no field of equine sport medicine, no endurance-oriented veterinarians, no "how-to" books. The popular "Natural Horsemanship" training methods and well attended clinics that start new riders out correctly today were unknown. Terms such as aerobic and anaerobic were virtually unheard, as were electrolytes, nutritional supplements, heart monitors, water bottles and even fanny packs that the modern-day endurance rider depends upon so completely.

I usually rode *Marinera well in excess of a hundred miles a week. I very simply rode the proverbial tar out of a horse that had too much heart. It is my hope that the love lavished on her in later years made up for an ignorant but enthusiastic rider, the worst possible combination for a horse with such drive. In the beginning years with *Marinera, I was not a perceptive enough horsewoman to look into her eyes and see the fatigue forced upon an animal whose spirit would not quit. It was she that taught me that the eyes are the single most important bellwether in determining a horse's general well being. In subsequent years I have made it a habit to accustom myself to the changing moods of a horse by focusing intently on the eyes.

After six months of arduous training, we drove to Lake Tahoe once more. With Verne waiting apprehensively at the finish line to see whether I did his favorite breed justice, *Marinera successfully cruised the Tevis Cup Trail and we finished proudly in the top 20 percent. Her strange gait was witnessed by many for the first time and the off-hand remarks compared the action of the forelegs with that of an egg-beater. They could laugh, but I know who had the smoothest ride that day.

*Marinera was a highly tense mare, however, and while physically she seemed to take the long distances in stride, her eyes told another story. She was an emotionally exhausted horse. I have always felt a tired horse was not a crime (I am tired at the end of a ride too), but an exhausted horse is. I adored this horse and when it came time to return her to her owner, Verne's client, Bob saw my anguish and purchased her. As inexperienced horse buyers we soon learned that once a seller recognizes that a person is considering a horse he has for sale, he immediately talks about the "other people" interested in purchasing the same animal. This stampedes the buyer into a quick decision during which the asking price is never questioned. Horse transactions are usually cemented by the heart and not the brain and *Marinera had intoxicatingly found a secure place in my heart. She was mine and I could not have been happier than if I suddenly owned Alexander the Great's famous Bucephalus or Man Of War himself. I had my *Marinera.

After her second Tevis Cup Ride, I looked into *Marinera's eyes again and saw once more, not a physically tired horse, but a mentally defeated horse. I was exploiting an animal I loved. Somehow my buckle was a bit tarnished. I decided that she would be more suited to a ride of a shorter distance. At that time I did not have the experience to know that a slow 100 mile ride is frequently kinder on a horse than a fast 50. There is a difference between a weary horse and a spent horse, depleted of any energy reserves.

There had been a previous 50-mile ride staged, but there were no plans to continue it. You rode the Tevis or you stayed home. So,

Photo by:
Charles Barieau

*Marinera at Emigrant Pass on the 1968 Tevis Cup Ride.

with the help of the Castle Rock Horsemen's Association, I started the Castle Rock Challenge Ride, the oldest continuous 50-miler
in the country. I could not wait a whole year for the next Tevis Cup
Ride so I was solving my problem with this new enterprise. Since
no one in the Horsemen's Association had ever been to an endurance ride, I was given free rein in organizing the competition,
and I attacked the project with great zeal.

The course was plotted, the trail was flagged so no one could
possibly go astray and the day was set. The location was to be Coe
State Park on the east side of the Santa Clara Valley. And yes, the
mustard still bloomed in the foothills. The park ranger had been
most cooperative and the completed entry forms I had sent out to
all the past Tevis Cup riders piled up on my desk. It was immediately apparent that people welcomed the shorter distance. It was
a volunteer effort by many association members and our expens-

es were limited to printing costs, the monitoring veterinarian's fee and the dinner provided for all the riders. The entry fee covered these expenses.

The date was set for mid-April 1967. It should have been May! A freak snowstorm put several inches of snow on the park floor and the ranger said he could not allow the ride to take place. In his mind, but most certainly not in mine, the trails were dangerous. Some riders could not be reached in time and arrived at the ride site only to be turned away at the park entrance. It had been a colossal blunder on my part to have not included on the entry form space for an entrant's telephone number. Six riders from Nevada made the seven or eight hour trip to the ride site only to be turned away without even a chance to unload their horses. My apologies were received graciously and all six returned a month later when the new date was set. The ride was finally held and all went well with the second scheduling.

Photo by: Charles Barieau

On the second running of the ride, *Marinera carried me to a
third-place finish against tough competition and then received
the Best Condition Award. The veterinarian team makes an evaluation of the first ten horses to cross the finish line and then selects
the one they consider to be in the most superior physical condition to honor with this special award. It was the prize I coveted
more than any other. Once again, though the distance was shorter, the look in her eyes was of a distressed animal. As my affection
for this giving animal grew, I reluctantly realized that I was continuing to misuse her. Within a year I retired her from long-distance riding. It was not all altruism. She was pulled from a ride at
the half-way mark with a case of thumps.[2] In addition, some
moldy hay had made a heave line appear on her side, a sure sign
of a respiratory problem, and she never regained the lung capaci-
ty that she had had earlier.

The Castle Rock Challenge Ride ride continued in the year 2000
to be one of the best attended and best known 50-mile rides in the
United States. I happily turned the chairmanship over to others
after the first year, and the Frank McCrary family has staged it
since the early 1970s.[3] A far better route now took it from near the
shores of the Pacific Ocean, through the redwood forests of Big
Basin State Park, ending back at the starting line in camp. The in-
ception of this ride seemed to be a catalyst for others who felt the
attraction of long distance riding. I think they decided that if I
could pull off a new ride successfully, so could they. Within the
next couple of years there were more and more endurance rides
throughout California and Nevada.

I continued my weekly retreats to the Santa Cruz Mountains
where I would disappear for the day with *Marinera. She was a
happy horse without the excitement of too many other horses
around and her exuberant spirit on such occasions gave me some
of the most joyous rides of my life. In all the 24 years I owned her,
I never had her shy, rear or buck. She fell only once in the thousands of miles we shared and that was when I was cantering her

in a sawdust covered arena. It had rained and the subsurface was wet. Her legs slid out from under her and she went down on her side. I was still on when she popped up and therefore can truthfully say that I never went off her in the almost quarter of a century that she showed me the world from her back. We rode in the winter, spring, summer and fall, in the early dawn and in the moonlight and she always gave me her best. She never cared to ride in groups. They always went too slowly for her and she became agitated when held back. If I were to pick one horse that had the most influence on my life, it would be *Marinera. She was a truly remarkable animal.

With *Marinera retired, my annual dilemma returned. I MUST have a horse for the Tevis Cup Ride and $350 bought me my first purebred Arabian. Chagitai had been my introduction to the Arabian breed and now I owned one. Rumadi was a freckled grey with the classic Arabian conformation—pretty dished face, short back, lovely large eyes, excellent head carriage and a wonderful arched neck. He was fun to ride. He loved to spook and shy at imaginary monsters on the trail, but my balance was good in those days and I managed to stay on top of him. I found a used English saddle[4] which fit him well and it gave me more freedom of movement than the heavier, more cumbersome western saddle I had been using.

I now was boarding two horses at some expense in the Santa Cruz Mountains. In order to justify the expense, I kept hoping that maybe Bob would ride with me. But I never asked him. Then one day he said, "If two of them are going to eat, two of them are going to work" and, lo and behold, he climbed on his first horse at age 52. Rumadi was not an easy horse to ride because he jigged and pranced when headed for home along with engaging in playful sideways spooking whenever it struck his fancy. I did not want to discourage Bob so I decided to forego any but the very basic instructions. Rumadi had a tender mouth and Bob put little pressure on the reins for fear of hurting him. The two survived each other and became a nice team. It worked well. I would ride *Marinera and Bob would ride Rumadi around our local mountains, which serve as an excellent training ground for bringing a horse to top form. Then, because I had retired *Marinera from competition, I usually rode Rumadi on two or three endurance rides a year.

Endurance riding in the early '70s was gaining in popularity and there were now several rides within a day's driving distance. Bob voiced no desire to compete, but Rumadi's ability, plus my better absorption of the subtle nuances of the sport, soon allowed us to compete with the "big guns." He took me to my first endurance win, a 50-mile race. It was heady stuff for me. The exhilaration was tremendous and I felt I had gained respect in a field that I dearly loved. And, I had a good horse full of Tevis Cup Ride potential.

There are several ways of approaching the Tevis Cup Ride. You can attack it as a glorified trail ride you hope to survive or you can accept it as a challenge to see how closely you can come to the top. Those that choose the latter soon find that if you are going to do well you have to think and "ride smart." Of the 250 entries you can assume that approximately 10% or 25 riders are going to see how well they can place. Of those 25 who start out with high ambitions, probably 10 will fall by the wayside. Either they or their horses will be found wanting on that particular day. But another 10, who suddenly find themselves doing better than they expected, who had started out with no personal ambitions except to just finish the ride, will suddenly find themselves propelled into the upper echelon. It is an awakening and is when "riding smart" becomes important.

Among 250 riders on a Tevis Cup Ride you can find every personality type on the trail with you. Your personality will determine how well you do that day. Listening to your animals is the most important job you have for the next twenty-four hours. The ones who focus on their horse and the trail, the two most important things in your life that day, are the ones who rise to the top. Experience teaches you how to play the game as well. It took me 16 years to get my 1,000 mile buckle representing 10 successful completions. I was disqualified 6 times in those years. But I have now completed my last 14 attempts without a pull. Somewhere along the way I learned how to play the game. I had proved to myself that mentally and physically I could achieve my goal. I had beaten the trail more times that it had beaten me.

One of the lessons I learned is that you ride the trail in segments. When you start out in the morning, your objective is Robinson Flat, 35 miles away. When that hurdle is met and cleared, you ride the next segment. Each successful passage to the next goal, builds your confidence. When you mount your horse at the start of a 100 mile ride, you have to remember that pacing is the name of the game—pacing consistent with the signals your horse is sending to you as a focused rider.

I entered Rumadi in four Tevis Cup Rides. He was excused from two for lameness, one which was temporary and no cause for concern and one which I considered non-detectable. I also learned something more important. On his second Tevis Cup Ride in 1970 we were disqualified at the 85-mile point of the 100-mile trail when we were in fourth place. The veterinarian said he "looked as though" he was going to go lame. In 37 years of riding endurance and 27,000 miles of competition, only twice have I considered the veterinarian's call unfair. This was the first. Afraid of appearing pushy, I did not ask for a second opinion, which, in retrospect, I should have. Trailered back to the Auburn Fairgrounds, I lunged Rumadi in tight circles and could not produce a single false step. He was a sound horse and I am still bewildered by the veterinarian's call. But I had no regrets. Just starting that adventure over the Sierra was worth every penny and every minute spent in preparing for the ride. The training and conditioning of the horse was sheer pleasure.

In spite of that disqualification, I consider it one of the best rides of my life. Rumadi was perfection that day. He skimmed the ground, zestfully attacked the mountains, proved his desert heritage by ignoring the heat and never took a misstep. He was having as much fun as I was. The important thing I learned was that personal satisfaction does not have to come from reaching the finish line or winning the approval of others. I thought I had ridden Rumadi well, and, though we failed to complete our mission, I considered his performance stellar. Rumadi and I had it right that day.

On only two occasions have I ever felt totally in harmony with a horse over the course of the many years I have enjoyed their good company. They were very fleeting but haunting moments, perhaps lasting less than 10 seconds, but indelibly imprinted upon my mind. Once was with *Marinera in the woods. We were alone and for a few breathtaking seconds at a canter, I knew I was riding her as well as any horse could be ridden. It was as though the two of us had lost our individuality. We had become a single identity. We were balanced; we were in unison and the energy flow between us was complete. The second time was with Rumadi during the course of an endurance event. We were coming down a gradual slope into a clearing with an old weathered ranch barn ahead of us. It was a scorchingly hot day and the green grasses of spring had dried and turned the oak studded hills to a golden brown. The trail curved to the right around the dilapidated building's collapsing fence line as it leveled off and then climbed again. Rumadi was in an extended trot, taking great long thrusting strides in his excitement over the competition with other horses. He came off the slope and into the level curve as a horse at liberty would, moving freely. I ducked low under an overhanging oak tree branch, but my timing and balance were perfect. My weight upon his back was not baggage for him. In the turn I leaned properly and I was his partner. As he started to shift his balance from the down hill slope to climb once more, he broke into a canter. It was a beautifully smooth transition from one gait to another. The horse and I were synchronized and the personal communication I felt with this animal was fleeting, but my elation at the experience has remained with me ever since.

I feel that if a horse and rider go down the trail together for an extended period, the two of them will figure out what works best in much the way that water seeks its own level. Endurance ride photos tell me that my riding posture could be pretty soundly criticized, and rightfully so. I tend to hunch my shoulders and lean forward farther than most riders. Most events have photographers on the trail and, when I see one ahead, I sit up straighter, throw my shoulders back and smile. When I get around the corner and out of sight, I return to my more comfortable, but incorrect, form. I do not feel that a riding instructor would claim me as a student. I had the first riding lessons of my life at age 70. I ached afterwards so decided that I would let my gray hair bail me out. I was simply beyond the point of learning new tricks.

Rumadi taught me a lot about horses. Unlike *Marinera, whose disposition was not suited for endurance, he was born to do what I was asking him to do. He loved to race down a trail. He was a tremendous natural athlete with a strong desire to run with the herd. However, a problem was looming that, at that time, I was not experienced enough to solve. The adrenaline rush Rumadi received from competition was making him almost unmanageable and he became increasingly difficult to handle. The starts of rides were becoming frightening for me. He had a tender mouth and the metal bar I put in it could stop him easily. But my efforts to slow him resulted in his prancing, dancing and spinning in circles. He knew when the horses gathered at the predawn start line that this was the day he would race. He was not particularly competitive or trying to beat the other horses. He reminded me more of a hyperactive child on Christmas morning who can't wait to open the gifts under the tree. He could not stand still. My horse savvy at that time was very limited and I failed to find a solution to the problem. I had never had a riding lesson and there weren't any clinics, seminars, videos or horsemanship classes of the sort that can prepare one for a better start today. I know I could have done far kinder and better jobs with *Marinera and Rumadi if I knew then what I know now. But someone had to be the teacher and someone the student. I was the latter.

Bob and I now had two horses that we thought were no longer suited to the sport I wanted to pursue—*Marinera because she was physically impaired and Rumadi because he was intimidating me. But the two horses, stabled in the same corral, had become good companions and I continued to ride one or the other several times a week and to ride with Bob on the weekends. Life was good.

My endurance ride cravings were fulfilled by the friends I had made in the sport. I was offered horses by others and continued to get my "fix" by competing on borrowed horses. The satisfaction was never as great, however, as riding a horse I owned, trained and conditioned by myself. I was still participating in the Tevis Cup Ride every year and had by then completed three or four Virginia City One-Day Hundred Milers. Bob's crewing was my salvation and his patience during long hours of waiting for me in the heat of summer and the cold of winter in outlandish places on distant trails was frequently vital to my success. So it was actually a rather well thought out idea Bob presented to me one day. Lo and behold!! He wanted to ride the Tevis! Or maybe he had simply had a "bellyful" of crewing.

The year was 1976 and he was a 58-year-old man with a goal. The horse he chose was a new acquisition. Beau was a Morgan/Arab cross and sort of a good-natured fellow, but not particularly inspired on the trail. He did his job, but not with the enthusiasm of *Marinera or Rumadi.

Mounting up at Squaw Valley at 5 A.M. during the full of the Indian Riding Moon,[5] the annual Tevis Cup Ride date, Bob dismounted 23 hours and 45 minutes later at the Auburn Fairgrounds. He had made the 24-hour deadline with only fifteen minutes to spare. It had been a long day and night but Beau had become a Tevis Cup horse and Bob had his silver buckle! It just doesn't get any better than that!

By happenstance, Bob rode the last ten miles of the trail with two teenage girls, the daughters of two well known endurance families. Riding along the American River in the moonlight, 20 hours away from his 5 A.M. departure from Squaw Valley, he watched while they giggled and laughed and promised him to secrecy as they lit cigarettes and puffed away. He marveled at their apparent lack of fatigue while his own body screamed for rest. When finished, they generously offered Bob one of the many sticks of gum they were stuffing in their mouth in hopes that the tell-tale tobacco smell would not be detected by their parents at the finish line. As far as Bob knows, the conspiracy worked and he exchanged knowing looks with them at the award ceremony the next day. Their secret has been guarded well, but if by chance they read this story, they will know who they are.

Bob's Tevis Cup completion record was now far better than mine. With this one ride, he could claim he had a 100 percent completion rate and mine was only about 60 percent. I had started the ride thirteen times but had found the finish line at Auburn only eight times. But more importantly, I had a husband who could identify with my passion. He had experienced the trail first-hand and no longer visualized it from my descriptions. And he had his silver buckle with the raised Pony Express rider dashing across the prairie. It was shinier than any of mine, for I had been disqualified that year and learned the game from the other side— waiting at the finish line for my rider to appear.

Was Bob as hooked as I by his first endurance ride? No, and he certainly didn't sleep with his buckle under his pillow as I had. He is much more level-headed on this subject. He can take it or leave it. He has completed about 14,000 miles of endurance riding by my side. His interest in the sport has been in the many new places it has taken us. I am far more interested in the behavior of

Photo by:
Charles Barieau

Bob Suhr crosses Cougar Rock on his first endurance ride, the 1976 Tevis Cup Ride.

the horse and why he reacts in a certain way to a certain stimulus. Bob is a total non-disciplinarian and I have never seen him strike a horse or become angry at one, or any animal for that matter. Nor does he feel the need to cry into their manes. I still do. As for feeling ten feet tall, he has never felt the same exhilaration at a finish line found that I have. I re-ride every ride for days afterwards. Perhaps better adjusted than I, he goes on to other things.

I have said many times that endurance riding is the sport that takes the humble and makes us feel ten feet tall and then when we get up there, it has a way if reversing our direction dramatically. The downward plummet can be quick and sudden. On one particular ride I came home with three trophies. Ten feet tall? Well, not exactly.

I went to this particular ride with a well-conditioned horse,

RIDE NAME _____    RIDE DATE: _____    DISTANCE:____    RIDER #

RIDER NAME:_____WT.DIV._____

HORSE
NAME:_____AGE:_____BREED:_____SEX:___COLOR:_____

JUNIOR RIDER [  ]    SPONSOR:_____

Mark at points of concern (can use contrasting color at final exam)
_____

**PRE-RIDE (FIRST) EXAMINATION**

Pulse_____

Resp._____

Temp._____

**POST-RIDE (FINAL) EXAMINATION**

Pulse_____    Heart
                 Recovery
Resp._____     Index

Temp._____

| Parameter | ABCD | Comments | Parameter | ABCD | Comments |
|---|---|---|---|---|---|
| Muc.Membranes | | | Muc. Membranes | | |
| Cap. Refill | | | Cap. Refill | | |
| Jugular Refill | | | Jugular Refill | | |
| Skin Tenting | | | Skin Tenting | | |
| Gut Sounds | | | Gut Sounds | | |
| Anal Tone | | | Anal Tone | | |
| Muscle Tone | | | Muscle Tone | | |
| Back/Withers | | | Back/Withers | | |
| Tack Galls | | | Tack Galls | | |
| Wounds | | | Wounds | | |
| Gait | | | Gait | | |
| Impulsion | | | Impulsion | | |
| Attitude | | | Attitude | | |
| Overall Impression | | | Overall Impression | | |

Signature of Examiner:_____    Signature of Examiner:_____

Elimination Cause:_____    Elimination Cause:_____

The 2001 Del Valle Vulture Venture Ride used a typical vet card that the rider must carry with him at all times during the ride. This horse "report card" is graded before the start of the ride, at each vet stop during the course of the ride and at the end of the ride. Grades of A B C & D are usually used to indicate the horse's condition. The front side of the card, as shown here, has a diagram where any surface lesions, swellings or past injuries can be noted.

| NAME: | | | | | | |
|---|---|---|---|---|---|---|
| **RIDER #:** | | | | | | |
| CHECK | | | | | | |
| ARRIVAL TIME | | | | | | |
| PULSE TIME | | | | | | |
| HOLD TIME | | | | | | |
| OUT TIME | | | | | | |
| Muc. Membranes | | | | | | |
| Cap. Refill | | | | | | |
| Jugular Refill | | | | | | |
| Skin Tenting | | | | | | |
| Gut Sounds | | | | | | |
| Anal Tone | | | | | | |
| Muscle Tone | | | | | | |
| Back/Withers | | | | | | |
| Tack Galls | | | | | | |
| Wounds | | | | | | |
| Gait | | | | | | |
| Impulsion | | | | | | |
| Attitude | | | | | | |
| Overall Impression | | | | | | |
| Comments | | | | | | |
| Heart Rate Rec. | | | | | | |
| Examiner | | | | | | |
| Elimination Cause | | | | | | |

The back side of the vet card shows the arrival and out times at the vet checks during the course of the ride. The veterinarians will look at the grades the horse received at the earlier checks to see how the horse is performing. If his examinations shows that the condition of the animal is deteriorating and the grades are too low, he will disqualify the horse from further competition and the rider will not be allowed to continue.

primed for glory. My competitive juices were flowing nicely and I had great expectations. My horse and I were ready to hit the trail and show everybody a thing or two. After I returned home, my daughter, Barbara, called to see how the day went. I told her "I won three trophies." She enthusiastically replied "Wow, Mom. That's great! You must have had the fastest time and received best condition too! But what was the third one?" I explained to her that she was quite wrong. The trophies I came home with were the Turtle Award for the last to finish and the Hard Luck Award because my horse went down in a slick spot and gave me a full body mud bath. And the third? Ah yes, the trophy for the Oldest Rider!

I still have those three trophies and, while I have not displayed them prominently on the fireplace mantle or on the coffee table for the edification of others, they have not been forgotten. I never start a ride without remembering them with dismay and silently hoping "never again."

## Chapter Eight

# *To the Mountains*

*And God took a handful of southerly wind,*
*blew his breath over it and created the horse.*

Bedouin legend

In 1973 we had been living in the small Santa Clara Valley town of Saratoga for twenty years. Our children were nearly grown with our daughter, Barbara, graduated from college and newly married. Our older son, Rob, had recently returned from his tour of duty with the Navy off the shores of Vietnam and had returned to school. Our younger son, John, was also in college. The house seemed emptier and lonelier than it had ever been. I loved my wonderful community and our friendships were fulfilling, but I wanted to have more than the city lot with neighbors on all sides. My discovery of the annual Tevis Cup Ride had been made nine years before and it was still the high point of my year. Now I wanted to have my horses in my own backyard, not boarded elsewhere. Everyone is familiar with the adage "You can take the girl out of the country, but you can't take the country out of the girl." My rural upbringing had deep roots.

Several years earlier, Bob and I had found the perfect spot while riding *Marinera and Rumadi on a Sunday afternoon. Sixty-nine acres of undeveloped property lay at the end of a dirt road, two and a half miles from a county road with no homes in that distance. We bought the property, dug a well and were now ready to build the home which we have occupied since 1973. I, with no training, decided to be the architect and promptly designed a home from which the horse pasture could be seen from almost every room. We were now "over the hill" both figuratively and literally, or so I thought. Our new location was in redwood country on the western slope of the Santa Cruz Mountains rather than the eastern slope and the town of Saratoga. After almost a half century in the Valley of Heart's Delight I was leaving, but not without some meditative regret. I was different now as was the paradise of my youth. The silicon chip reigned where a valley floor covered with fruit blossoms and wild mustard had once delighted the senses. My desertion was a significant turning point in my life, but the Valley and I had both changed.

We now overlooked Monterey Bay and as my 50th birthday approached, I visualized this as a retirement home. Being almost half a hundred years old seemed terribly ancient and I thought of my life as being on a down slope with the best years behind. Empty nest syndrome, mid-life crisis, whatever, I was there. The children were on their own and the dinner table was now wistfully set for two instead of the larger family to which I had become accustomed over the past years. Bob went off to work each morning and I gardened, painted and wall-papered. We had no neighbors except for a "hippie" enclave nearby. They were young, idealistic and occasionally wore clothes. With my horses as my sole companions, I embarked upon an exploration of the mountains that would become my backyard for so many years. We were about six miles from the Pacific Ocean as the crow flies. When I was riding, the shoreline mist sometimes crept in and blocked the sun. It was airy and transparent and it was fun to run for home

and see if my horse's legs could get me there before the fog en-
shrouded trees began to drip on us. On a summer evening the
pasture in front of the house provided the crickets' summertime
sonata that I had missed with city living. I felt as though I had
come home.

Our life in the Santa Cruz Mountains gradually became truly
horse-oriented. We named our property Marinera Ranch and the
road on which we lived, Marinera Road. My father did not live to
see my departure from the Valley of Heart's Delight, but he loved
redwood country and I like to think he would have approved. My
mother, now in her mid 80's, lived alone in the large ranch house
where she and my father had raised their children and lived so
many years. Progress and the encroachment of city outskirts had
greatly reduced the acreage left in pears, but the immediate vicin-
ity of my childhood home was still surrounded by the orchards
that had been so good to my family. The handwriting on the wall
was very legible, however. When building our new home in the
mountains, Bob and I added a small apartment with a kitchenette
in case my mother should need a place to live. But it did not come
to pass. She came to visit frequently for several days at a time and,
with a tone of pronounced resignation as she watched me clean
corrals in my blue jeans, said that she was happy for me. She fed
the horses carrots and patted their soft muzzles and I knew she
understood at long last. It was terribly important to me.

With our emphasis on training Arabian horses for endurance
competition, *Marinera's talents were being wasted. So we put her
to work having babies. Starting when she was 13 years old, she
gave us nine foals. One of her daughters, Danzarina, gave us seven
more. With two exceptions, I was there for the birth of each one.
They were prized moments. The owner's anticipation increases in
direct ratio to the swelling of the mare's belly. And then the apprehension begins.

Mares traditionally have their foals at night. There is simple
logic to it. Wild horses usually journey in their search for food

during the day and bed down at night. The expectant mare will distance herself from the herd, deliver the foal and rejoin the group before it has had time to move on when daylight arrives. In the wild, the horse being a prey animal, must be able to escape quickly from danger. A mare is at her most vulnerable during the birthing process. In the nearby group environment, and under the cover of darkness, she finds safety. Delivery must be quick and the foal must be on its feet and ready to run with the herd within a few hours. Labor seldom exceeds more than an hour and if delayed much beyond that point, the health of the mare and the unborn foal are in jeopardy. It is an indication that the mare is having a difficult, and possibly fatal, delivery and that both the mare and foal will suffer the consequences of an incomplete or strenuous birthing experience.

And so, at Marinera Ranch, the "great foal watch" would begin. About two weeks prior to delivery I would oversee *Marinera's every movement from my architecturally superior, horse-watching-designed home. Picture windows made it all possible. At night I would desert Bob, grab my sleeping bag and bring *Marinera into the barn. Reading for awhile under the dim barn light bulb would occupy an hour or so and then, about 10 o'clock, Bob would arrive at the barn door with a glass of wine for each of us. When the glasses were empty, his devotion to me was compromised by thoughts of the comfortable bed in the house and he would leave. Curled up on the bales of hay, I slept fitfully and learned for the first time that horses snore. The longest period of "barn sleeping" for me was eleven nights. Mostly I was a little more on target as to the delivery date, and just a few nights would pass before I was richly rewarded.

The miracle of birth is not confined to the human race but must be shared with the stirring of new life in the animal kingdom. The delivery is quick and sudden with the foal's debut frequently completed within twenty to thirty minutes after the first signs of labor. From my perch on the bales of hay I silently observed the wonder of it all. The emergence of the foal, wet and slick, is greeted almost immediately by a muted maternal nicker on the part of the recumbent mother. The foal's chest cavity expands with its first sweet breath of air; flattened, tiny wet ears go forward and the newly born responds with its own soft nicker. The bonding has begun and the beauty of the moment demands respect of the person privileged to observe it.

*Marinera's deliveries were all quick, easy and, with one exception, without incident. I thank her for that. Her babies were up on four spindly legs and nursing within an hour of birth and doing their awkward baby paso gait soon after. In the morning, when the barn door was opened, she would strut out proudly with her joyous prize by her side. Up and down the driveway, the spindly legs began the first of the many miles they would travel in a lifetime. It always caused great excitement among the other members of the Marinera Ranch equine community and it was a noisy affair as each horse personally greeted the newcomer with loud whinnies. It was enough to awaken Bob who would come out on the deck and observe the scene with relief. He could have his glass of wine that night in the comforts of home, not perched on a bale of hay under a dim light bulb.

*Marinera broke all the rules only once. She liked her mountain home and I never worried about her straying so gave her complete freedom to wander at will without confinement. In the summer she preferred to be on the ridge beyond the house where the summer breeze kept the flies away. One year, mistakenly thinking I still had several days before beginning my annual barn vigil, I checked on her occasionally during the day, but not as diligently as I should have. Unable to see her from the house, I went outside to investigate. She was nowhere in sight. Going to the last place I had seen her, I found the telltale signs that she had given birth, but saw neither mother nor child. The area was particularly steep and the path in the tall grasses that the mother and newborn had taken was plainly visible. I pictured a tragedy and went in pursuit. The foal, in its efforts to stand for the first time on wobbly and un-steady legs, had obviously had trouble balancing on the steep hill-side and started a descent into the forest below with *Marinera in desperate pursuit. About 200 feet below the birthing spot was a fence and my distraught mare was there, hysterically running back and forth with no offspring in sight.

The newborn had slipped under the fence and its struggles to stand were carrying it further into the thick woods. With the hill-side too steep for me to stand, I slid down on the seat of my jeans in search of the foal, digging in with my heels to slow myself when necessary. Another 300 feet and the baby came in view. Though still wet from the birth, I could see he was coal black with a white star dead center on his forehead. He was a mirror image of his sire, our stallion Carioco. He struggled repeatedly to stand, but each effort resulted in a further plunge down the mountain. I grabbed at anything—slippery legs, head, neck, tail—and could halt his progress briefly but simply was not strong enough to do any more than that. Desperate and helpless, I knew no one could possibly hear my calls. His chances of survival were in my hands alone and I had to find a way to save him. I took off my jeans and, using them as a sling, wrapped them around his tiny form. As I embraced his slick body, I could feel his heart racing and, when he stopped his exhaustive struggling for a moment, I could see the minute frame heave with each distressed breath. While I clutched the cuffs of my jeans, the colt's thrashings continued to pull the two of us downward. With the laws of gravity on his side, I was no match for this slippery, struggling 85 pounds. We reached a more heavily forested area and our descent was slowed some-what as I braced against the trees. Finally I was able to wedge the foal in among some tree trunks and heavy shrub growth. I wove branches in among his legs in an effort to prevent his struggle to rise again. He appeared drained from his efforts and his scram-bles to gain his feet became more feeble. Leaving him (and my jeans) behind, I grabbed at vines and tree branches and laboriously pulled myself back up the hill, sometimes slipping back and having to seek a less steep route. Reaching the top, I was now as out of breath as the colt I had left behind and, knowing that minutes counted, I wondered if my efforts would all be in vain.

*Marinera was still in a frenzy on the other side of the fence. Breathing heavily from my exertions, I patted her in what I hoped was a reassuring fashion, but I think only confirmed her anxiety. I feared she would try to run through the barb wire, but I knew that there was no way she could keep her footing on the steep hillside anymore than I had. Would she break through the fence and crash down upon her own foal and crush him?

I ran to the house and started phoning neighbors. Starting with the closest, I listened impatiently either to interminable ringing or a busy signal. I needed help so desperately and I knew the fate of this foal depended on my using my head. My frustration increased. Didn't anyone care about my predicament? I felt very much abandoned and alone as my efforts to reach anyone seemed hopeless.

I was now calling people I only recognized by name. Would the fire department come for such an emergency? Should I call the animal shelter? No, it would take them much too long to get here. And then, my anxious dialing brought a response. I had found a friend whose husband was with her and the two of them said they would come immediately. I grabbed a blanket in case we needed a sling larger than my jeans, or, perhaps I feared the worst. Would a tiny body need covering?

Donning another pair of jeans for decency's sake, I met my rescuers in the driveway. The three of us formed our plan. My friend, Nancy Caldwell, and I would go in search of the foal, while Nancy's husband, Mike, stayed behind to formulate a plan for retrieval if the foal was located. Repeating my slide down the hillside, and with Nancy not far behind, we found our foal with the jeans still wrapped about his small, distressed body. While his breathing seemed shallow, the rapid beats of his heart could not be concealed by the thin layer of hide covering his rib cage. The birth fluids had dried from his body and he was easier to handle as I pulled my jeans from beneath his body and replaced them with the blanket sling. Nancy and I examined him carefully and decided that he had not broken any bones or otherwise injured himself in his thrashing. We guardedly lowered him foot by foot farther down the precarious slope to an old logging road, taking turns bracing ourselves below him to catch him in case he slipped out of our larger sling.

In the meantime, Mike, with apparent total disregard for the future of his Datsun station wagon, and fearing he could not turn around, backed down the narrow and rough road until we met. The three humans, with the spent foal, now carefully lifted and placed in the back of the Datsun, triumphantly returned her latest progeny to *Marinera. She was grateful for the reunion and the delayed bonding took place as Nancy and I held the now severely weakened foal upright so that he could nurse. We watched the progress of his first urgent sips of the life-giving mother's milk as they coursed down the long slim neck. His strength returned rapidly and I relaxed. I knew all was well once again. I will never understand what possessed *Marinera to give birth in the middle of the day on the side of a hill and I never quite trusted her after that episode.

The day was not over, however. That night, *Marinera's daughter, Danzarina, decided to give birth also. This production, thankfully, was uneventful and the next morning I had two new babies to parade proudly up and down the driveway. A week later another daughter of *Marinera's, Carolana, delivered. Three foals in a week's time increased our horse population considerably, but the care of them was not a chore. It was truly my delight.

In the period from 1975 to 1988, 21 foals were born at Marinera Ranch. The Peruvian Pasos were much in demand and bringing good prices. My usual program was to keep the foals until weaning time, about six months, then offer them for sale. By that time

The "Over The Hill" foal . . . Dignatario.

Ad from The Peruvian Horse Review.

they were halter-broken and had been taught to lead, to allow their feet to be picked up, to be brushed and loaded into trailers. Some of them sold fairly rapidly; others were kept until they were several years old. I gave each one up with reluctance, but only once did I regret a sale. The new owners of one weaning filly had little horse experience and did not seem to have the natural know-how that is so important for the well-being of the animal. The foal was later sold by them to a friend of mine and a good home was assured and I was at ease as to her future.

Small breeders become very attached to their babies as they handle them on a daily basis. No two ever respond in exactly the same way and it is up to the trainer to build confidence and use discipline at a rate a youngster can absorb. Push too fast and the animal becomes stressed and fearful. Too slow or repetitious a program will result in boredom and lack of concentration and the instructions are not retained. There is a balance and the trainer needs to read the colt's moods. Once again I found the answer by looking into the eyes. A pattern for each individual would become apparent and I found my youngsters very willing to please as long as they understood what I was asking.

Selling a horse whose birth you have witnessed is a bittersweet pleasure regardless of how much the sale swells the pocketbook. The partings are frequently sad and there can be few sights more forlorn than a woman watching a trailer drive out of her yard with one of her foals setting off for an unknown future over which she no longer has any control. It is even harder to see the older ones leave. If more than a couple of years old, I had given them some saddle training. The longer they were around, the more attached I became and I was unable to part with two of them. They are now in their mid-20's and still reside in the barn where they were born.[1]

> *The stomachs of mares are treasure chests*
> *bulging with gold.*
>
> Emir Abd-el-Kader

## CHAPTER NINE

# American Endurance Ride Conference

*Movement is the primeval element of his being,*
*joyous movement in the wide spaciousness of freedom.*

Hans Heinrich Isenhart

While I was busy raising foals at Marinera Ranch, there was great activity in the endurance world in the early 1970s as more and more rides were being staged all over the country. In 1972, in order to bring some sort of uniformity to the sport and to offer more protection to the horses, an organization called the American Endurance Ride Conference, Inc. was formed. By sanctioning only rides that met its criteria, the Conference offered a central clearing house for ride dates, ride results and a point system for recognizing top performances culminating with a year-end award banquet and ceremony. Record keeping became an important part of the Conference's interests and an educational program for establishing veterinarian guidelines was instituted. We also recognized that if our sport was to continue and grow, we must make an effort to see that trails were preserved for our future use.

The founding group was primarily made up of Auburn endurance enthusiasts. This was most appropriate because Auburn was, after all, where Wendell Robie had accepted the challenge of a 100 mile ride in the mid-1950s. I was asked to join the group and write some articles to promote the sport and was given the title of publicity director. As such, I sent articles to various horse-oriented magazines extolling the virtues of the sport, with some added information concerning the early development of endurance riding in America. Wendell Robie had by then become known as the *Father of Modern Day Endurance Riding* and 'his' Tevis Cup Ride was thought of as not only the toughest ride in the world, but also the most prestigious. It became the prototype for future endurance riding in the United States as well as internationally.

As interest in this burgeoning sport grew, much discussion ensued about purported inequities and how we could make our sport more fair. The concept of weight divisions, separating lightweight and heavyweight riders into two competing groups, was gaining popularity. I was against it. I wanted every rider to enter the sport with whatever assets or liabilities he or she had. I did not want us to founder on too many rules. In 1973, I sent the following article to be published in the AERC's Endurance News, the organization's monthly publication.

> In a regimented, departmentalized and regulated 1973 society, beset by federal, state and local rules governing which way we turn, how fast we move, when we pay and how much, a refreshing sport has developed. It is called "endurance riding" and to the uninitiated it is insanity. But to most who have tried it, it is an insidious sport which charms while taking captive its willing victims who discover that the thrill of a good ride on a good horse is one of life's greater experiences.
>
> Basically, the underlying philosophy of endurance riding is for the riders, each coping with his own particular assets and liabilities, to get from here to there as quickly as possible while maintaining the physical condition of the horse at a high level capable of passing veterinarian standards designed primarily to protect the horse from either overeager or unknowledgable riders. At the moment, endurance riding is a run-away success with more rides being organized each year and more riders participating. But because it is attracting wide attention, it is also subject to much criticism. The main outcry seems to be that the lightweight riders have

an unfair advantage over the heavyweight riders and therefore some sort of handicapping system should be initiated in order to make the rides "fairer." This is certainly indisputable—ALL OTHER THINGS BEING EQUAL. But all other things are not equal and that is why the heavyweights such as Bud Dardi, Ed Johnson, Pat Fitzgerald, Nick Mansfield and Cliff Lewis have made it to the top.

What are some of the other inequities? Can we, with the driving of this one wedge, weight divisions, prevent the driving of more until this young and crazily wonderful sport is diluted and subdivided as our society today, until the original is no longer recognizable? This is what we have to decide and this is where every real endurance rider should give some careful thought. If we really want to make it "fair", perhaps we should consider some other aspects.

1) Pro versus Amateur
   This is an obvious division because it is apparent to all that the owner of one horse who works five days a week in an office and makes a couple of rides a year does not have an equal chance against the man who spends seven days a week working with many horses and makes a dozen rides a year.

2) Newcomer versus Experienced Rider
   I believe endurance success is divided this way: 1/3 horse, 1/3 rider and 1/3 luck. Put an experienced endurance rider on a fair horse and 90% of the time he'll beat a novice on a superior horse. You learn something new at each ride. The more rides you make, the better your chances the next time out. So to be equitable, should we give the novice more time or a head start?

3) Familiar versus New Trail
   Should a rider making his first trip at a particular ride get a head start over those who know the trail and can pace their horse accordingly? The confidence of both the rider and the horse are greater on a familiar trail.

4) Homing Instinct
   Should horses who live and are trained at the finish line end of fifty and hundred mile trails compete with horses who have no idea whether the ride ends fifty yards or fifty miles away? Endurance riding is largely mental on both the part of horse and rider. Homeward bound horses quicken their gait.

5) Age versus Youth
   Some particularly athletic riders have found tailing out of canyons and dismounting and running down a hill a tremendous help in saving wear and tear on a tiring horse. But what about the older rider whose body does not accept this kind of punishment as well? Some horses are going to have to pack their riders the whole way. So should we have some sort of age division or let the older riders start earlier?

6) Veterinarian versus Layman

Now that so many veterinarians are starting to compete, should a layman's knowledge of a horse be pitted against their knowledge? More than a few riders would have paid dearly for the medical expertise which would advise them as to whether a sudden lameness could be "walked out" or whether further exercise could do more or perhaps even permanent damage. Signs of fatigue detected by the expert eye can easily escape the less knowledgeable. That is the reason for having the rides supervised by skilled veterinary practitioners.

7) Arabian versus Other Breeds

Each year seems to bring further proof that the Arabian horse is superior to other breeds in this particular field of horse activity. Should we give the non-Arabian riders a head start down the trail? Sound ridiculous? It doesn't to the people who don't have an Arabian.

8) Conflict of Interest

Should a ride chairman compete in his own ride? Should a member of a judging veterinarian's family be allowed to ride? Should a judging veterinarian be allowed to enter his horse with another rider into competition?

The questions are endless and range from the serious such as the weight problem, to the absurd, such as white horses do better in heat than dark ones so let's have categories according to color and weather conditions. What seems unimportant to one rider may make the difference between winning or losing for another rider. Are too many rules better than not enough? Are we over organized or under organized? Should we try to cover all the bases by making a rule to meet each contingency? If we correct one inequity, how can we continue to ignore others? Is the ultimate goal to make enough rules to correct all the disparities until we have done such a fine job of handicapping that all the hundred or so horses in a ride cross the finish line simultaneously? A grand and glorious sight? I doubt it. We do know, however, that the rider has choices. He has the freedom to choose the endurance route which says the glory goes to the guy who gets from here to there the fastest regardless of size, shape or color. Or he can go to Competitive Trail Riding where provisions have been made for the differences in age and experience of the competitors. It is the rider's choice. I do know that not much in life is truly fair and so it is with endurance riding. But maybe we have to accept our sport as it is-a totally unfair, but glorious endeavor which will die if diluted by other than a few minimum rules which should be designed primarily with the welfare of the horses in mind. In its present form, endurance riding is admittedly unfair; it is addictive; it is expensive; it is exhausting. It is also exhilarating and rewarding. Why else would we all be there?

It was my first real effort at trying to steer the sport in the direction I thought was correct. I received many comments, mostly positive. But there are now, in the year 2001, four weight divisions—featherweight, lightweight, middleweight and heavyweight. My efforts were very much in vain in spite of the fact that many others feel as I do.[1]

There were other factors threatening the harmony of the infant sport. There was a widening rift developing between the American Endurance Ride Conference and the Western States Trail Foundation. Two organizations, which should have been bonded by a common interest, were at swords' points due to strong personalities in both groups. The American Endurance Ride Conference was setting up guidelines that were to apply to all sanctioned AERC rides. The Western States Trail Foundation, on whose Board of Governors I served, sponsored the Tevis Cup Ride. It had been running its own show for seventeen years and was not about to have anyone else dictate how their ride should be run.

To persons such as myself, whose introduction to the endurance was on the Tevis Cup Trail, but who believed the ever-expanding sport had to develop with some sort of standardized guidelines, the rift between the two organizations was painful. My efforts to bring the two closer together were mostly unsuccessful in the early years, but a good working relationship has now been established. At this time there is mutual respect and people with more foresight are in charge of both organizations.

The newly formed Conference was administered from people's homes with volunteers devoting untold hours keeping the fledging organization afloat. In 1975 I received a phone call from the AERC's first president, Phil Gardner, saying he needed help. I became secretary-treasurer and record keeper almost overnight, as well as keeping my job as publicity director. I once again proved my wisdom as an architect for I was able to sit at my desk doing Conference business and look over my left shoulder at my horses in the pasture below. It was truly a labor of love for I was living and breathing the sport that meant so much to me, though it seemed mostly vicariously. We did not own a trailer; Bob was working full-time and there was much to do in developing our

Photo by: Charles Barieau

Pre-ride briefing—Castle Rock Challenge Ride—1972.

Photo by: Charles Barieau

The start of the 1972 Castle Rock Challenge Ride.

property and resolving the endless details of a new home. We also found it impossible to leave our home and animals unattended while we went off for a weekend's ride.

I learned a great deal additionally while serving as the AERC's annual Convention chairperson over a three-year period. We decided to move the end-of-the-year award ceremony and banquet out of local Auburn/Sacramento area hotel dining rooms to the Nugget Hotel in Sparks, Nevada as a two-day conference. I dutifully made all the arrangements from handling the convention reservations, mailing out brochures, lining up the speakers, choosing the menus and providing for decorations. When my children came for Christmas dinner one year, they found the house littered with AERC business and the afternoon was spent stuffing envelopes and licking stamps. Santa was put on hold. Each convention was a full year's project on my part and demanding enough that I learned a great deal. Fortunately, I found Bob's background in organizational work my greatest asset and he bailed me out many times when problems arose with which I had had little previous experience.

By 1978, the job of secretary of the organization soon became much too large to be handled by a volunteer. By the time the decision was reached to have a full-time paid secretary, who would handle the convention too, I felt very much like a pro. By 1978, the conference that I had happily participated in since its founding, was keeping track of 135 rides[2] nationwide and more than 1,500 members. To be active in the development of a young and growing sport was fascinating and the groundswell of acceptance and enthusiasm shown by new converts was extraordinary.

There was a second issue to which I took strong exception. Many riders were demanding rides of a shorter distance than 50 miles. Fearful the sport would become diluted, I played a part in having written into the by-laws that "an endurance ride by definition is not less than fifty miles" (later reworded). The concept of shorter rides of 25 to 35 miles being run in conjunction with the "endurance" rides of 50 miles or more and calling them "limited distance rides" was accepted by the AERC and incorporated into the by-laws.

In the year 2001, many years after the initiation of limited distance rides, the issue is still a hot one. My feelings remain unchanged. In my opinion, a ride of under 50 miles is not a test of endurance. However, I have become a fan of the shorter limited-distance rides as an excellent way to introduce young horses and new riders to the sport on a less demanding level. It also offers aging riders and horses a step down to a less demanding level of long distance riding. Limited distance rides give people an opportunity to try the sport and then make a personal decision as to whether to set their sights on higher mileages, stay where they are or decide the sport is just not for them. Hopefully they will graduate to the longer distances and become endurance riders with all that title implies. On a final note, the entry fees of limited distance riders help bail out some rides financially.

With the risk of alienating some, which I regretted, I made it clear that I did not think a ride of 25 miles required a tremendous amount of training or dedication. I do not feel its participants have really proven a whole lot. I can swim, but I am not an Olympic swimmer; I can jog, but I am not a marathon runner; I can play chopsticks on the piano but this does not make me a pianist. I do not think this makes me a lesser person. It means, for whatever reasons, in these particular fields I am not a shining star. I can ride 50 or 100 miles, however, and this does make me an endurance rider.

There is another category of riders—those who because of personal problems, physical disabilities, time restraints or other reasons cannot opt for the longer distances. They love their horses; they love the trails; they want to be a part of the whole scene. So limited distance rides of up to 35 miles have given them this opportunity to do so. I, probably sooner than most people now en-

Photo by:
Pat Mitchell

Eight year old Stephany Ashley and 26 year old Lawlifa
enjoy a 25 Mile Limited Distance Ride.

gaged in riding 50 or 100 miles, will be forced to cut back to limited-distance rides. (I just seem to predate most of the people riding.) When that time comes, I hope that God will give me the
grace to accept the fact that I am no longer an endurance rider. I
am a former or ex-endurance rider just as Joe Montana is a former
or ex-football player. When I can no longer compete effectively, I
hope that common sense will tell me to accept it as graciously as
possible, whether I like it or not.

Our lovely old Arabian mare, Lawlifa, produced 15 foals.
When we decided she had more than done her duty as a broodmare, she did her first limited distance ride at age 25 with 8-year-
old Stephany Ashley on her back. By definition, it was not an endurance ride and, therefore, did not make Lawlifa an endurance
horse or Stephany Ashley an endurance rider, but we were all

proud of what the old horse and the young girl accomplished. Then as now, I feel that the beauty of our sport lies in the simplicity of each rider participating with his or her own unique assets or liabilities under demanding standards of performance. If riders cannot find fulfillment here, they should seek it elsewhere.

CHAPTER TEN

# Off to See the World

*When he gallops, he humiliates the lightning.*

Horse of the Sahara by E. Daumas, 1863

When Phil Gardner, the AERC president, asked me to act as the Conference's secretary in 1975, I did not realize that the typewriter on my kitchen table would lead me to South Africa to endurance ride. A letter from Mr. Dirk deVos, the secretary of the Endurance Ride Association of South Africa, inquiring about endurance riding in America, started a continuing correspondence. It culminated in the Orange Free State on July 15, 1980 when, with the playing of the Star Spangled Banner, the American flag was raised by an American Field Service student in Bob's and my honor at the beginning of their three-day National Endurance Ride. Our pride and emotions at that moment were deep and stirring.

When the invitation to attend their National Endurance Ride arrived, I semi-seriously said to Bob that I wanted to go to South Africa to endurance ride. His reply was, "Tell them you'll come if they have a horse for me too." They did and we were on our way!

We were told the first endurance ride was held in South Africa in 1973 with 21 participants. When we took part in 1980, they had staged 16 pre-rides which culminated in the National Ride. In sharp contrast to the United States, the sport in South Africa was recognized and partially subsidized by the government and supported by the Army. As the first people from another continent to participate, we received a royal welcome, I am sure in part because it was a period when South African athletic programs were being boycotted by many nations. Twenty-three persons met us at the airport upon our arrival in Johannesburg. We thought we were tired from the 25-hour journey, but the wining and dining that followed erased the fatigue. For the next eleven days we were their guests, living in their homes, eating at their tables and riding their horses. Our pretty rondeval, or guest cottage, next to Mr. deVos' home in the countryside between Johannesburg and Pretoria, was comfortable, private and surrounded by exotic plants.

Mr. deVos had the largest Arabian horse breeding operation in South Africa in 1980. His pride in his stock was evident as he took us from corral to corral to see his animals. Our introduction to the horses we were to ride came the next day. Mine was a grey Arabian mare, Sudarik Orolet, owned by Mr. deVos. She was about 14 1/2 hands[1] tall, a comfortable size for me. She had an illustrious endurance career, liberally sprinkled with wins, best conditions and Top Tens. I could tell the burden was upon me not to waste her talents. Her hair seemed rather coarse to me until I realized that it was midwinter in South Africa and that under the shaggy winter coat was a really lovely mare. Bob's horse, equally shaggy, was a tall, very lean and leggy part-bred[2] Arab gelding belonging to Johannesburg businessman, Mr. Len Cilliers. His name was "Breker," apparently due to a habit he had of 'breaking away.' He was well named as Bob was to find out. Breker had finished in eighth place in last year's National Ride and was a free-moving audacious animal with an aristocratic air about him.

Before leaving for the ride a scene took place in Dirk's home

From Die Volksblad, July 16, 1980. (Bloemfontein Newspaper)

Julie on Sudarik Orolet. Bob on Breker at the site of the 1980 South African National Endurance Ride. Fauresmith, Orange Free State, South Africa.

that would be familiar to every ride manager and secretary in the United States. Our host's home was completely taken over with ride brochures, trophies, ride lists, veterinarian sheets and past ride records. Ride secretary Janet Glyn-Cuthbert, an English woman but longtime resident of South Africa, was as harried as her American counterparts just prior to a ride. A quick glance at an early entry list showed a field of 41 geldings, 17 mares and 19 stallions. This was a much higher proportion of stallions than we have on our rides. Over half of the entries were Arabian or part-Arab. The rest were Boerperds, descendants of horses brought to South Africa during colonization and registered as a specific breed after the Anglo-Boer War, nondescripts which compare with our grade[3] horses, a small native breed called Basuto ponies and one striking Appaloosa that held the record for completing all six previous National Rides. Seventeen of the entries were from the South African Defense Force, trained and ridden by members of the Army. Because horses are used for border patrol,[4] the Army considers endurance riding a keen test of their breeding stock. They watch closely to see which bloodlines excel and keep careful records to guide their future breeding programs.

A nine-hour jaunt with seven horses and three vehicles brought us to the ride site, the town of Fauresmith in the Orange Free State. The countryside reminded us of many parts of Nevada where we have ridden, basically flat with rocky sandy soil and little vegetation. The town was small and the weather was bitterly cold. We had exchanged midsummer California for midwinter Southern Hemisphere. Our small rooms in the local hotel had no central heating and we slept under six blankets. If the wind did not blow, it warmed up for a short time during the day. Back home, under very different weather conditions, it was Tevis Cup Ride time and, for the first time in 16 years, I, sadly, would not be there.

We learned that the National Ride was 210 kilometers, or 130 miles, in three days. A 50-mile loop was to be made the first day. The same loop would be done in reverse the second day and the third day would consist of a 30 mile shorter loop. The same horse and rider must finish all three days to earn a successful completion. Having never asked a horse to come back three days in a row under competitive circumstances, we looked forward to the new experience. We felt we would be as sorely tested as the horses and hoped we would represent our country well.

The National Ride is a week-long celebration and definitely the major endurance event of the year. Families, crews and riders had ample time to become well acquainted as the locals welcomed us. The ladies of Fauresmith prepared three meals a day and the Army entertained with a Braii (barbecue) followed by a dance under a starlit African sky. Church services were conducted in English for our benefit by Chaplain Hedley Smith, an Army entry in the ride who also entertained us in his home. A slide show presented by Professor Grosskopf, the head of the University of Pretoria's Veterinary School of Medicine, showed on the screen, by means of graphs, the results of extensive blood tests they were conducting on endurance horses.

The same evening we gave a similar slide show to tell of endurance riding in America. We decorated the walls with American endurance ride pictures, Tevis Cup charts, Castle Rock Challenge Ride brochures, AERC literature, decals and rider lists. It made us feel at home. The questions flew at us, and Bob did some bragging by telling the gathering that I had won my last endurance ride in the United States two weeks previously. Orolet's owner, Mr. deVos, now my good friend Dirk, confided to me that he expected me to do equally well on his horse. The pressure was mounting and I was not entirely comfortable knowing so many eyes would be watching my performance.

The National Ride had a staggered start. We were sent out to the "field of battle" in small groups. Dirk, very much the director in charge, decided that I and his ride secretary, Janet Glyn-Cuthbert, should stay close together and I was more than willing to follow his directions. I was on a strange horse on a strange trail in a strange country and my self-confidence was eroding rapidly. A few miles into the ride Orolet's stride became even and unbroken and I found the rhythm pleasant. My saddle was comfortable and the stirrup length adjusted properly. A difference of even half an inch in the length of the stirrup can affect my riding and my comfort level, but, in this case, I was able to achieve the balance that I felt would hinder my mount the least. The sandy and rocky trail was being mastered by a horse who wanted to run. I had come so far and I already knew it had been worthwhile.

Orolet was eager and anxious, pulling and thrusting against the reins and insistently demanding that I release the pressure on the bit in her mouth. She wanted the freedom of her head so that she, not I, would set the pace. She was a savvy mare and had been here before and so I acquiesced. She knew her job and instinctively settled into an efficient gait. I don't think I was too familiar with the term "aerobic" at that time, but I knew what it was even if I did not have a name for it. A horse at a gallop breathes in unison with its stride. As the forequarters are lifted off the ground to make the next stride, the body organs shift to the rear and air is pulled into the lungs. When the horse lands with its front feet, the back end is elevated to bring the rear legs under and the organs shift forward and the pressure on the lungs helps to expel the air. The faster the pace, the more rapidly this process takes place. The horse becomes anaerobic if high speed is maintained and exhaustion soon follows.[5] Orolet was in a hurry but she was very much in tune with her body. I respected her judgment and quickly realized that she needed little guidance from me to remain aerobic.

Janet's horse and Orolet were stablemates and they worked well together. Janet and I also seemed to have hit it off nicely and she guided me and encouraged me. Dirk, obviously nervous over sharing his best horse with an unknown rider, met us at the veterinarian checkpoints and administered to his animals while I stood by and hoped I was winning his approval. When we crossed the finish line this first day, we had a riding time of 3 hours and 32 minutes for the 50-mile course. We had averaged over 14 miles an hour. We had covered nearly the entire course at a gallop, and, while not physcially exhausted, I suffered severe back pain that I had never before experienced. A flat course is very much harder on a rider (and a horse) than a course with ascents and descents and winding mountain trails. The latter requires both you and your horse to constantly change your body position to stay in balance. This movement allows certain muscles to relax as others are brought into play. The flat South African course forced my body into maintaining the same position for lengthy periods. When I dismounted I tried to hide my distress from Dirk, but he was alert and quickly saw that I was in trouble. He did not have to voice his concern. I saw it in his face.

Bob's first day was eventful when Breker lived up to his name and broke away while Bob was making a tack adjustment. Somehow, being on foot in the middle of South Africa wasn't exactly what Bob had planned, but with the cooperation of others, horse and rider were reunited. He enjoyed his day and the company of a young South African teenager who rode with him. The Stars and Stripes were lowered when he came in from the trail and he was touched by this gesture on the part of our South African hosts.

Dirk came to visit Bob and me in our tiny hotel room that first night and brought with him another man who claimed he could fix my back. With no questions asked, the solution was sharp and to the point, a needle in my rear. My back did feel better the next morning and I never inquired about the substance in the needle. Somehow it seemed better not to ask since it was now a *fait accompli*. But I felt sure that if the next day's ride treated my spinal column to similar stress, I was going to hide it from Dirk.

I had a second visitor that night. One of the ride veterinarians came to our door and reminded me that I had come half way around the world to make this ride and that if I continued at high speed, he felt Orolet would not last the three days. Dirk, her owner, as well as my patron in South Africa, vehemently disputed this and told me that I was to ride Orolet up to her abilities. I felt uncomfortable about the situation. Dirk had generously loaned me his favorite horse and had been our gracious host. I wanted to do my best for him, and particularly for his horse in which he took so much pride. On the other hand, I did not come this far to fail and I was willing to heed the veterinarian's advice and slow down in order to enhance my chances of finishing all three days. I thought a night's rest would help me sort it all out, but sleep came only fitfully and I rose in the morning in as much of a dilemma as the night before.

I left the next day's starting line with very mixed emotions. Dirk, the horse's owner, was telling me to ride faster. The veterinarian's words were ringing in my ears. The important thing to me was to complete the 130 miles. Speed is a risky business in this sport. It reduces the chances of finding the finish line. I was very willing to listen to the veterinarian who had shown the concern. And it was not just my aching back that was calling for a more conservative pace. I simply wanted to return to the United States with the completion of this ride successfully achieved.

Janet and I were still riding together and her companionship was terribly important to me. She was not only my confidant by the second day but also my security blanket. I needed her. Janet had been following Dirk's riding instructions for many months before I appeared on the scene. I questioned the wisdom of continuing at the fast pace and her answer was "Dirk knows what his horses can do." I knew she was right and I leaned over Orolet's shoulders and gave her the signal. We would gallop.

Orolet readily agreed and I increased the speed of her trot until she broke into the gallop that had wracked my back the day before. I knew if I were to survive, I would have to allow my mind, so filled with desire to do well, to take control of my body. It did and we finished this second day's ride in 3 hours and 39 minutes, only 7 minutes longer than the previous day. I had now ridden 100 miles in approximately 7 hours of riding time. Janet and I and our deVos horses were running up front with a top place finish not out of the question. I had 30 miles to go the next day and I had to somehow draw the mental and physical strength needed to complete the task.

Bob completed the trek on Breker at a slower pace the second day, but both he and the horse looked splendid. He was having a good time and later that night we spoke of the race and I confessed my concerns. Could I sustain the pace that Dirk and Orolet had set for me? Bob and I had been provided with excellent mounts; now we must prove our own excellence.

The wind blew through the night and, once again, I slept little. Trying to find a comfortable position was not possible. The breakfast table, laden with bacon and eggs the next morning, had little appeal but I knew I had to gain strength from some source and so I ate what I could and hoped it was sufficient to fuel my body for this one last effort. One Hundred Miles behind us. Thirty to go. Should I try for a top finish to please my host or slowdown to increase my chances of finishing?

Orolet was presented to me by her groom the next morning, already saddled (a luxury to which I was not accusotmed in the United States) and looking far fresher than I. As I settled in the saddle, I still had not come to grips with my quandary. From my perch on top of her, I looked at Orolet's neck stretched in front of me, the wispy mane carefully groomed. I looked between her ears at the start line and felt her eagerness and wondered how such a small frame could pack so much energy and vitality. The veterinarian who had warned me to slow down checked us visually as we passed. I did not want to meet his eyes, but I was drawn to them. By his expression, a half smile, he admonished me—"you are not through yet." I am not a poker player, but I sensed unspoken words on his tongue. Somehow I felt that, in truth, he was rooting for me.

Dirk's "thumbs up" this third day was more than a gesture. I was not to waste Orolet's talents. The message was clear. "Give her her head and let her run." Janet and I started out on this final leg of the South African National Championship Ride running very near the top. The four of us, the two horses and two riders, were now a smooth working tandem machine. We would be galloping this last 30-mile stretch as we had the first 100 miles. Or so we thought. Ten miles from the finish, at the last check point of the ride, Janet's luck ran out. She swallowed her disappointment and urged me on when she had to drop out when her horse was lame in a forefoot. We had matched each other stride for stride for 120 miles and I marveled at fate which decided an English woman and an American woman, both doing and loving the same thing, should meet on the African veldt.

But my race was not finished. Orolet, now missing the companionship of her stablemate and racing buddy, was on her own. I worried she would lose heart and fail to perform at her best as she had for so many long, dusty, and rocky miles. And perhaps I needed Janet so that I would not lose heart. I need not have worried about Orolet. She knew her job. She was a trooper, and the loss of her equine companion did not change her attitude or discourage her. Could I win this ride? I left the veterinarian check point in second place. Somewhere out ahead of me, with only a few miles left to go to claim victory, was a young man in his twenties on a horse we needed to catch.

From my position leaning far over Orolet's withers, with a back that had failed me completely, I glanced from the road ahead to the road beneath. Looking at the ground over her left shoulder, I saw this wonderfully slender and graceful leg in flight appear beyond it. The knee joint straightened as the leg stretched out and then the hoof, reaching out for more ground, came into view. It dropped and hit the dirt path. The thrust and the momentum of Orolet's body hid it from my view as it disappeared under her body to prepare for the next great stride as the burden switched to the other foreleg. With but few miles to go, she was running harder now than she had at any time during the race. The memories of my races on Dick against imaginary opponents among the rows of pear trees returned. Except my rival was not a youthful fantasy. He was very much real and just a short distance ahead of me.

Stories such as this are supposed to end with a valiant mount's efforts claiming victory by a nose in the last few strides. But Charles Lord's riding time of 9 hours and 36 minutes put Orolet and me out of the winner's circle by five minutes. Our time of 9 hours and 41 minutes for 130 miles was the fastest race I would ever ride. I was obviously given a super horse and let her (and Dirk) down by not riding her up to her potential once my back

From the Blomfontein, South Africa newspaper Die Volksblad 7/16/1980
Photographer: Unknown

Julie Suhr and Sudarik Orolet finishing the 130 Mile South African
Endurance Ride in the Orange Free State—1980.

started to bother me. I felt sure that, for the first time, Dirk and I
were now in agreement. Orolet should have won.

Bob's good horse brought him home in 11th position, but Bob
felt that his mount was a better animal than that indicated. The
lost time on the first day could not be made up in a race where
minutes counted.

Fifty-seven riders successfully completed the three-day ride.
An endurance ride of more than one day was unknown in the
United States at that time and the new concept of consecutive
days in the saddle under competitive circumstances gave me a lot
to ponder. Perhaps this was much more a test of endurance and
horsemanship than our one day rides with which I was more familiar. It was a new concept, but twenty years after our African
adventure, in the year 2001, there are probably 25 of these multi-

day rides in the United States under the auspices of the American Endurance Ride Conference. Increasingly popular, they offer a serious course in horsemanship. The horse that is over-ridden the first day, does not return on successive days. The rider has to make continual assessments of his horse's condition with a trained eye capable of noticing subtleties in a horse's look or behavior. In South Africa, Dirk and Orolet's groom evaluated her when she was not in the field. In this country, my horse is under my supervision and I make the judgment calls. I prefer that.

The South African National Endurance Ride culminated in a parade of finishers the afternoon of the third day, the American flag, along with that of South Africa, waving over our heads. I had been so concerned with my own performance that I had spent little time observing the other horses that had successfully completed the ride. I watched with tremendous satisfaction as 57 horses passed in review, with each looking as though a fourth day would not have been too much to ask of them. The less fit horses had been weeded out by the veterinarians over the three-day period.

Some of the awards were presented at this time, and Bob was surprised to find that his group of four was to receive the award for the team to complete the ride in the shortest time. Orolet had earned me the honor of being the senior rider over 50 years of age to complete the course in the fastest time. I overcame my pride long enough to accept the trophy. Orolet also won the trophy for the first purebred Arabian to finish. Her second-place finish gave recognition to a gallant little mare who so willingly bore a stranger upon her back without complaint for 130 miles. How I wished I could have tucked her in my suitcase and brought her home to California.

The festivities culminated with a dinner-awards ceremony and Bob and I received our belt buckles, the first ever to leave South Africa. We proudly brought home certificates of achievement and a gold medallion[6] for my second-place finish.

The most frequently asked question by the South Africans was

"How do our horses compare with yours?" It was a difficult question to answer. The three-day aspect of their endurance ride was different than anything we had encountered in America and I firmly believe their horses are every bit as good as ours. We have very few flat rides in America so it was hard to draw comparisons. Certainly legs, hearts and lungs that can gallop for fifty miles can be trained to climb. While I did not check each horse, my general impression was very favorable. The 70/40 pulse and respiration requirement, lowered from previous years, slowed the ride and the veterinarians thought the animals looked the best ever.[7]

The thirty horses disqualified were mainly ruled out for lameness. I think there were two cases of metabolic problems resulting in poor recovery rates. The big difference I noticed was that of riding style. Almost without exception, the riders sat back in the saddle at the gallop, even when racing up short inclines. The habit of grabbing the mane and pulling one's weight forward had not been adopted, but I think if the riders were in steeper country, they would choose this method. I saw no sore-backed horse so do not fault their style, only comment on the difference.

The winning horse, a part-bred 6-year-old gelding, was awarded the Best Condition trophy, a double victory for his rider, Charles Lord. How I would have loved to have had Orolet win that honor for the generous Dirk who put the well being of his favorite and best horse in the hands of a stranger from another land.

Having come so far, we thought we should see more of the country. Bob explored the diamond mines in Kimberly and Table Mountain in Cape Town while I remained bedridden with the flu, restlessly trying to find a comfortable position for my still aching back. My recovery was rapid when presented with the chance to once more climb upon horses which only a few days previously I had sworn to forsake forever. We took two days to pony-trek in the Drakensberg Mountains. Sturdy native horses took us over countryside experiencing the worst drought in its history. We were saddened on the second day to look back over the country we had covered the previous day and see flames and smoke engulfing the scant feed left for the animals. From horseback on another day in a game preserve we spotted a white rhinoceros, loads of impala, wildebeest, a giant kudos and innumerable wart hogs. I was glad the horses' legs, not ours, were on the ground.

With this first journey abroad, we established some long-lasting friendships and found that, as in America, the South Africans love riding, jogging and running marathons. My fondness for Dirk was solid. His love of his horse and his chosen sport must have made it agonizing to watch someone else at the helm while he stood upon the ground. And I shall not soon forget Janet who kept assuring me the vet check was just around the next bend in the flat, seemingly endless road. And there was Len who also gave up his horse that Bob might ride. But most of all, our gratitude goes to Orolet and Breker, whose eight sturdy legs never faltered.

An American Field Service student, studying in South Africa, raised the American flag each morning as Bob and I went out on the trail.

## CHAPTER ELEVEN

# Unlimited Horizons

*Paradise on earth is found
on the back of a good horse.*

Arab Patriarchs

South Africa was our first foreign adventure. It triggered a wanderlust in us that we found difficult to resist in the ensuing years. Prior to that trip, journeying across Canada during our honeymoon 34 years before, and a visit to Mexico, were pretty much the extent of our foreign travels. In turned out that South Africa, however, was but a prelude. Our world was beginning to expand rapidly.

## ALASKA

Through a mutual friend we met a rider who included us in a rare journey. His name was Chris Lingar, an Army officer stationed temporarily in Alaska. He invited us to join his group of trail riders. When last minute scheduling problems arose, Chris was unable to ride, but he introduced us to a couple who would become close friends, Walt and Bobbie Holst.

Riding time is limited in our 49th state and Walt treasured the few months when the weather permitted him time on his beloved Arabian horses. With a group of friends, he planned a special journey. The gathering, in which we were now included, consisted of 12 horses and riders with three or four other people to drive the trucks and trailers loaded with our gear as well as our mounts. We wound our way caravan style up the Haul Road that parallels the great Trans-Alaska Pipeline to a spot just north of the Arctic Circle. Mounted the next day, we crossed the wide Yukon River, and proceeded to follow the large cleared swath around the pipeline. It was the one and only time people were allowed to use this route on horseback. At that time the pipeline was owned by six oil companies, but the land which it crosses was owned by the United States Government. It was the BLM that had granted us permission to follow its route south.

Photo: Courtesy of Walt Holst

At the Arctic Circle at the start of 120 mile trail ride.

This was not an endurance ride—no clock to beat, no burning questions as to placement—just a pleasure trail ride. Congeniality blossomed as both men and women, young and old, were doing what they loved most, guiding a horse down an unknown trail as new and exquisite panoramas unfolded. The Alaskan fire weed was in full bloom and it seemed a shame to trample the colorful display with our horses' hooves as we wended our way south toward Fairbanks at the rate of about 20 to 25 miles a day.

On one particularly windy and rainy night (it really could not be called "night." It never became totally dark), we sought shelter in an abandoned shack. The boards were loose, the nails long ago rusted out, and, through the roof's splintered shingles, we could see the rain clouds above. We heated our dinner over a small camp fire inside the well air conditioned shanty and were only partially protected from the weather. We made sure our sleeping bags were out of reach of the water that was only temporarily impeded in its downward path by the roof that lay between us and the opening heavens above. Some chose to sleep there also, but Bob and I pitched our tent on the tundra a short distance away. With our horses tied nearby in the half dark of midnight, we could peer out the tent flap at them and see their silhouettes, tails to the wind and rain.

While we slept one person was left to patrol around the camp. It was not so much that we feared danger from outside our little enclave as it was concern that a horse might break loose, run off and cause the others to escape also. I had my solitary shift from 12 to 2 A.M. and, as I walked my circles around the small encampment, I was accompanied by the shrill wind and the ominous rattling of the loose boards where the others slept. The horses, as uneasy as I, occasionally nickered back and forth as if to find comfort in each others presence, as I was finding in theirs. I was relieved when my shift was completed and someone else started their lonely vigil. By dawn, the skies had cleared and in the evening, twenty miles to the south of our eerie, wet and cold location of the

Following the Alaska Pipeline
toward Fairbanks in 1982.

Bob Suhr dressed for a day's
ride at the Arctic Circle, 1982.

Photo by: Bobbie Holst

Walt Holst was hardier than the rest of us!
Alaskan Pipeline Ride, 1982.

night before, Bob was swimming in bright sunshine in a shallow lake. It was a short dunking, however. The mosquitoes had little respect for man or beast near any body of water.

During our journey south, the oil companies, concerned about our proximity to the pipeline, sent a uniformed and armed guard to ride with us. He was a nice chap, but his experience with horses was limited and his comfort level even less so. After two days he remembered things he needed to do back at the office and from then on the oil companies monitored our actions by helicopter. They scanned us from the sky above five or six times a day to be sure we were not a threat to their oil bearing ribbon of steel. It is my understanding that they have successfully kept anyone else from repeating our trek.

Dr. Bob Dieterich, a veterinarian friend of our host, also checked on us by air several times. A private pilot with his own aircraft, Dr. Dieterich is involved in the management of the reindeer herds. He and his wife, Jamie, a microbiologist, developed the vaccine which he uses to inoculate the animals against certain diseases. A good friend of the riders, he landed on several occasions and joined us at meals after having taken care of any concerns the riders might have about their horses.

As we rode, and became closer friends with some of the riders, Walt Holst stood out as the most dedicated horseman of our group. He had many questions about the Tevis Cup Ride and it became apparent he harbored a dream of riding it someday. A year later he accepted our invitation to fulfill that desire. At the age of 70 he arrived at the finish line in Auburn after a very long day in the saddle. He returned to Alaska with the silver buckle that I had sought many years before, proof of his accomplishment on his first endurance ride ever. At age 76, Walt returned and rode one of our horses on his second endurance ride, again the Tevis. I regretted that on neither occasion was I able to provide Walt with a horse that could give him a ride commensurate with his horsemanship skills. They were good animals, but not the spirited, trail covering type he would have preferred. These are the only two endurance rides in which he has ever participated and I believe they remain among the highlights of his life. His license plate reads TEVIS-2.

Once again, endurance riding had introduced us to a fascinating personality who became our good friend. A few years ago, Walt, at age 80, decided there were simply not enough daylight hours in Alaska to do all the riding he still had in mind. So he and Bobbie moved to Montana where he continues to saddle up and sally forth almost daily for long jaunts exploring the Bitterroot Valley.


FRANCE

Contacts with French riders we met at a Tevis Cup Ride in 1984 led to an invitation to compete in their Florac 100 Mile Ride in Southern France. Once again, we were guests, accepting the hospitality of virtual strangers, sharing their tables and riding in their cars. Denis LeTartre was our genial host and his picturesque centuries old vine covered chateau was our residence for several days of riding among the vineyards and olive orchards in the area. And then, once more, it was off to the main event.

There were five American participants in the Florac 100 Mile Ride and the trend of exchanging horses and riders throughout the world was becoming more commonplace. People with foresight realized that the crawling infant sport had now risen to its feet and escaped the shores of America and was standing on its own in many different nations. The future would prove we were in unbelievably good company in France. In South Africa we were very much alone with no American compatriots with whom to share our experience upon our return to more familiar shores. In France, we were sharing the adventure with fellow Americans. Potato Richardson, who introduced us to Denis and helped us plan our trip, would become a Tevis Cup winner years later. In the

French countryside, our introduction to Valerie Kanavy gave no hint of future performances that would bring gold medals to our country as she twice became World Champion. Mark Dees, whose love of speed went far beyond that found on the back of a running horse, could hold a crowd entranced with his race car stories. Lost too soon to the world of fast horses and fast autos he loved so much, his ashes now mingle with the dust of the Tevis Cup trail and the waters of the American River that lead to Auburn.

Bob Suhr at a 100 Mile Ride in Florac, France, 1984.

Italian riders look at the mountainous terrain on the Florac 100
Mile Ride in France, in 1984.

Denis LeTarte, our host in France, watches as a veterinarian
checks a horse at the Florac 100 Mile One Day Ride.

A sixth person, American veterinarian Dr. Matthew Mackay-Smith, came as an observer. Matthew and I had made our maiden voyages down the Tevis Cup Trail together in 1964. Matthew reached safe harbor in Auburn. I barely left the dock. But nothing Bob and I encountered on the backs of our horses on the bluffs above the River Tarne, or in the gorges below, will ever be as harrowing as the trip from the mountains to the sea with Matthew. One hand on the wheel while gesturing animatedly with the other, foot on the throttle of an unfamiliar French automobile, he was determined to make his flight out of Marseilles. Anyone passing us would have seen my stricken and blanched face peering out the window from the back seat. But nobody had the chance to overtake us—the foot on the throttle saw to that. Perhaps it portended the future when this same determination saw Matthew cross the finish line in first place at two of America's premier rides in the same year—the Tevis Cup Ride in California and the Old Dominion 100 Miler in Virginia in 1995.

Back to the Florac 100, we gathered at the ride site in the small town of Florac in southern France a few days early and familiarized ourselves with parts of the trail. The horse I was given was named Marie and she was both larger and stronger than I really liked. I had my usual pre-race jitters as to which one of us would be in control. She settled down nicely, however, after the first few miles which included a steep climb. I had no further worries and as I began to relax, my fondness for Marie grew with each step. She was sweet and very willing. A lovely French couple had been assigned the job of crewing for Bob and me and dutifully met us at each stop and saw that both we and our borrowed horses had first class treatment. They worked around the clock to see that total strangers from another land were able to achieve their goals. The horse world is filled with such people who share vicariously the joys of riding.

From each trip I have some outstanding memories. In France it was toward the end of the 100-mile ride, when fatigue was overcome by wistfulness that the journey was about to end. We had started before dawn and ridden through the canyons forged by the River Tarne and then scaled the escarpments above. Single track trails in the early afternoon widened into two track trails and I could ride side by side with Bob. By nightfall we found ourselves in beautiful open fields of wheat which a brilliant moon illuminated to almost day-like conditions, an idyllic summer night in southern France. The crickets filled the air with the sound of summer that I had loved so as a child and, once again, a special moment was secreted in my mind forever.

Nearing the end of the 100 miles, we rode through the ancient, by American standards, town of Florac from which we had started so many hours ago. It has very narrow streets with stone buildings rising several stories on each side. The sound of the horses' hooves on the cobblestones echoed in the narrow passageways and we were suddenly taken back to the days of Dumas' Three Musketeers. We lacked the plumed hats and the clanking sabers but we felt every bit as triumphant. Three people leaned out their windows near midnight as we passed and called "Okay, Americans" and gave the thumbs-up signal. We returned the universal sign of triumph as we patted our horses. They had done so well and we wished that we were sure they knew.

As with our previous trips, a desire to see more of the country was all the impetus we needed for side excursions. Marseilles and Paris were included in our itinerary before we arrived home. The following year, we hosted a French rider, Pierre DuPont, and provided him with a horse to ride in the Tevis. We were eager to repay our debt for the many kindnesses that had been extended to us a year earlier.


AUSTRALIA

After we returned from France, I sorted through my mail at my kitchen desk in Scotts Valley to find a letter from the secretary of the Endurance Riding Association of Australia. Rather than inviting us to ride there, Patsie Sinfield turned the tables on us. She wanted to come to America to ride the Western States Trail Ride, now known worldwide as the Tevis Cup Ride. We invited her to be our guest and use one of our horses.

Patsie, prominent and very active in the sport of endurance riding in Australia, deplaned in San Francisco after her long flight across the Pacific. Whisked from the airport upon landing, we immediately thrust her into a fifty mile endurance ride which covered the last half of the Western States Trail. She proved herself the ultimate good sport. She left Australia in mid-winter and 24 hours later, in mid-summer California, shoved her foot in a stirrup and climbed aboard a new horse, smiled and successfully rode 50 miles. She was ready for the 100-mile junket across the Sierra. Several weeks later, we undertook the Tevis together and when the main event was over, she made our home her headquarters as she toured California. When she left, now as a good friend, she begged us to come to Australia.

We succumbed. A year later, by way of New Zealand and a ride on rented horses near Milford Sound, we finally arrived at Patsie's doorstep. I was introduced to the long distance mileage champion of Australia, Patsie's mule, Juanita. Much beloved, Juanita was loaded into the trailer, or box as it called in Australia, for the trip to the ride site in the small town of Taralga in New South Wales. The 50 Mile Taralga Ride was a large event for a small town and they coordinated their sheep trials with the ride weekend. We watched with fascination as each farmer put his dog, primarily Queensland Heelers, through an intricate course with barely visible signals; a slight nod of the head, a twist of a wrist, a whistle and these smart dogs, with a devotion to pure efficiency, performed at their best. Their singular focus as they crouched and held a band of sheep in position or herded them in the direction desired was remarkable to witness.

Once again, as in South Africa and France, the spirit was fes-

Patsie Sinfield with
Australian Long Distance
Champion Juanita.

tive. My endurance 'horse,' Juanita, trotted and ran the first 25 miles quite gaily, but slowed considerably the second half of the contest. She was a fun and exciting animal, a beloved character on the Australian endurance ride scene. From her back, and between her long, slim, elegant ears, I was able to view the rural countryside, smell the eucalyptus trees and get a real taste of the flavor of this "Down-Under" country. I looked in vain for kangaroos and koala bears but a visit to the Sydney Zoo produced the only sightings.

Bob was given a young Arabian mare to ride. She was fairly inexperienced and new to endurance riding and he found her difficult to control. He had a few questionable moments, but finished successfully, pleased that the mare had not been overly depleted by her extra gyrations during the early part of the ride. When the main event was over, we returned to Patsie's home with the wonderful Juanita in the trailer, munching contentedly, knowing she had put in her usual good performance.

It was with sadness we left Patsie, but at her suggestion we took a side trip to Cairns. Queensland's Great Barrier Reef gave Bob a chance for some good snorkeling and completed our journey but not without instilling in us a desire to see more of Australia in the future. I think it is possible to travel from Perth to Sydney by train and sometimes even an iron horse has appeal.

Upon our return home, and while reflecting on our three inspiring foreign adventures, it became apparent that endurance riding was bringing us new friends from around the world and we were doing it as inexpensively as possible by accepting the hospitality of others. Our airfare came out of our pockets, but once we arrived, we were taken into the homes of fellow endurance riders and the expenses were minimal. My time at the kitchen table as the AERC secretary was paying off with wonderful dividends in the form of newfound friends and chances to ride in many parts of the world.

We had now ridden endurance rides on four continents, North America, Africa, Australia and Europe, but the free ride was about over. The AERC had grown to a point where a paid secretary did the work and the letters which brought new horizons to us no longer crossed my desk. However, we had been filled with an insatiable wanderlust. We found that we were immediately connected to new acquaintances by sharing the same interests, the same love of horses, the same love of riding. But we were now wondering "What next?"

We had no plans for future rides away from home after our return from Australia. We had run out of overseas contacts, but the craving for adventure was now firmly entrenched in our psyches. It was then I made the noteworthy discovery that one can ride almost any place in the world using equine tour groups to make the arrangements.

I doubt anyone is more fearful than I am the first time I crawl on a strange horse. After 37 years of endurance riding I am still a hopeless insomniac before each endurance ride when I am riding my own horse. The thought of crawling on an unfamiliar horse in a new land brings on even worse attacks of sleepless hours of tossing and I ask myself why I undertake such ordeals. These moments of introspection disappear once the horse starts to move out. It is then I have the answer to my question. They say that mankind's greatest adventures start with the first step and that comes when I thrust my foot in the stirrup of a saddle on an unknown horse in an unfamiliar country. Little did I realize how many "first steps" were to follow.

Photo by: Charles Barieau

Riders are timed across the finish line and in and out of the vet checks during the course of the ride.

CHAPTER TWELVE

# Between the Ears

*The air of heaven is that which blows*
*between a horse's ears.*

Arabian Proverb

Those who love to fly want to look upon the world from the sky while those who love the open sea want to view it from the bounding main. Mountain climbers think the world is at its best when gazed upon from a peak high in the sky and there are those stalwart souls who feel the necessity of exploring much of it with their own two feet. Bob and I discovered a way we felt was superior to any of these. To be truly appreciated, we feel the world must be viewed between the ears of a good horse. And that is what we set out to do! Our first totally independent tour, free of any endurance ride or mutual friend connections, started deep in the heart of Asia.

## MONGOLIA

The brochure from Boojum Expeditions[1] in 1986 invited us to share adventures seldom experienced by anyone outside of Mon-

141

golia. Mongolia? We reached for the atlas. The decision was made within minutes and the deposit check mailed the next day. According to the leaflet we were to explore parts of Inner Mongolia on native Mongolian ponies[2] such as Genghis Khan used when he swept out across Asia and struck fear into all those unlucky enough to be in his path. We would be visiting villages unseen by foreigners previously and we would have to be able to adapt to sudden schedule changes. We should expect some hardships and be in good health. We had been duly forewarned.

Our group of a dozen Americans arrived in Beijing to the news that, due to a prolonged drought, the native Mongolian ponies were too malnourished to be ridden. The Chinese government, which then had jurisdiction over Inner Mongolia, solved the problem by confiscating the Mongolian polo team's horses. A long drive from China's teeming capital city left most signs of civilization behind us as we journeyed, not without some apprehension, to the junction where we would meet our horses and the Mongolian Polo Team which would accompany us. People and horses were assessed as to experience and riding skills and hopefully suitable rider/horse assignments were made. We were going to be sent out into the great grasslands of Asia on polo ponies that had never been out of an arena. Divesting ourselves of all earthly caution, and with silent prayers, we climbed aboard and the fireworks started. Some of the animals exploded with enthusiasm like Fourth of July skyrockets at the touch of a match. Many of us went in unexpected and unplanned directions before the horses settled back down to earth. Having survived, our confidence was shored up and our apprehension was replaced by bravado, some of it probably false.

Our large entourage consisted of twelve American paying guests, the Mongolian polo team that came along to supervise their horses, our American tour leader, a young English girl interpreter, a cook, a Chinese woman doctor, five Mongolian wranglers and several government officials. Closed to the outside world for many years, tourism was permitted in Mongolia only after the communists reopened the borders. The area in which we rode is a vast desolate plain and there was frequently nothing on the horizon in any direction except the immense unending grasslands of central Asia. It was difficult to discern in the landscape the fine line where land and sky wedded, but the sight jolted the recesses of my mind. Out of the past I recalled a Cole Porter song I had loved in the late 1940s. *"Give me land, lots of land, under starry skies above. Don't fence me in. Let me ride through the wide open country that I love. . . ."* I had to work to recall all the words, but little by little they returned. *"On my cayuse let me wander over yonder . . . and gaze at the moon until I lose my senses."* I hummed it repeatedly to myself as the verses once lost in memory returned to my conscious world. I visualized a cowboy, half a planet away riding night herd, becoming overwhelmed by the immensity of his surroundings as I was now by the milieu of Mongolia. His thoughts were put in words and music that I loved as a youth and more recently returned to popularity by Willie Nelson. They encompassed the world as did the sky above. *"Send me off forever, but I ask you, please, don't fence me in."*

Sometimes there were herds of camels, sheep and the Mongolian ponies breaking up the starkness of the landscape. All these animals were hungry, the drought had seen to that, and it saddened us. At night, after a day of riding, we sometimes slept in yurts, a tent like dwelling made of animal skins. More often we curled up in sleeping bags on the ground. On occasion, the government officials asked the people of the area to share their homes, humble by our standards, with us. This was a communist country and they did as they were told. Although it made us somewhat uncomfortable, their friendly smiles indicated they considered it an honor. We spent one night in a small habitation sleeping on a board about twenty feet long. Six of us were lined up like a cord of wood and it really didn't matter who was next to you. We were tired and dirty, and rest was our only concern. Surprisingly, daily hygiene, which in the beginning was sadly missed, became unimportant and a pan of water, a small bar of soap and a clean cloth seemed adequate for our needs. We were comfortable with the food provided, not our standard American fare, but to a hungry rider, it was welcome. Our liquid intake, however, was unusual. Told not to drink any water, we were provided with unlabeled green bottles of beer. Lacking refrigeration of any type, we soon became accustomed to beer that was "grassland" temperature.

Bob was the only casualty on the trip. In a small village, he organized a volleyball game between the tour guests and the members of the Mongolian polo team. I was the cheerleader and was expected to shake a crumbled Chinese newspaper in the air at the appropriate time while trying to get the throng of spellbound Mongolian onlookers to give rallying cheers. It was spirited competition with each side good-naturedly accusing the other of reaching over the net or committing some other serious infraction of the rules as played in our home towns the other side of the globe. In a burst of athletic enthusiasm, Bob fell and cut his knee while trying to spike the ball. The doctor made a great occasion of the incident and, as though preparing for a surgical operation, brought out her medical kit. With little Mongolian children staring in awe, she daubed his knee with iodine!

We always felt completely safe and, as the fair-skinned Americans, we were objects of curiosity. As we passed through small hamlets, the villagers followed us en masse wherever we went, including into the primitive community outhouses. The hit of our entourage of Americans was a statuesque blonde from Texas. Her leather jackets, adorned with rhinestones and colorful rawhide fringes, along with her gaudy boots, were a sensation. She was striking in appearance and, except when riding, was usually surrounded by the village children who would have cheerfully followed her without question to the end of the earth. Nor were the marvels of her charms lost on the older Mongolian males.

About a week into our journey, we were confronted by a thunderstorm. In the distance, many miles away, the black clouds and

the lightning flashes were clearly seen and heard. They were accompanied by an undercurrent of increasing apprehension by our
group of riders. As the sky darkened and the wind increased, we
hoped the ominous clouds would take their threat of a serious
drenching beyond our reach. It was not to be. Our jackets flapped
in the wind and the horses manes and tails were lifted and
whipped about by the first gusts that came from several directions. Our mounts became as uncomfortable as we when the del-
uge hit with no visible shelter on the horizon. Their quickened
steps splashed mud upon our legs and, when they turned their
heads, the whites of their frightened eyes were visible. The storm
vented its anger as if to tell us, the foreign invaders, that we were
not welcome. The tension in both the horses and the riders increased in proportion with the storm's fury and, though the
weather was not particularly cold, we all felt a chill at the uncertainty of our situation.

We were spared when a guide's keen eyes spotted a building in
the distance and a simple farmhouse grew larger as we peered
through the wall of rain. Neither we nor our horses needed any
encouragement to pick up the pace as we zeroed in on the shelter.
We descended upon an elderly man whose small living quarters
had barely enough room to keep our group out of the downpour.
He was quite short and, if he was astonished by the unexpected
and dripping guests who towered over him, he displayed an extraordinary hospitality for someone who probably never saw the
inside of a schoolroom. He made tea for the invading riders and
his graciousness was exceptional. In the corner of his bunk lay a
tiny lamb wrapped in a towel and beside it, a kitten tucked in one
of the folds. With no sign of sheep for miles around, we wondered
as to its origin, nor did we ever see the mother of the tiny ball of
fur, so mercifully protected from the elements by this caring man.

Communication was difficult, but the manner in which he welcomed foreigners into his modest home made our host a gentleman of exceptional grace. When the dark skies brightened and the
storm moved on to take some other errant travelers by surprise, I

wondered if the brief downpour would be enough to make the grasses grow again in the barren parched earth. I hoped so. We bid our adieus to this benevolent man with whom we could communicate only with smiles and gestures. Aboard our horses once more, we had traveled several hundred yards when I turned back for one last glance at this haven in the midst of the now drenched grasslands of Mongolia. Our host, silhouetted against the stark horizon, was growing smaller with each step of our horses, but he remained standing in his barren yard with a hand raised in farewell. I doubt he will ever forget the invasion of his modest living quarters by strangers who fleetingly, and with tremendous gratitude, descended upon him. The memory of his nearly toothless warm smile always brings an appreciative grin to my face.

Our farewell to our horses, and the polo team that had accompanied us, was somewhat pensive. We were all fairly certain our paths would not cross again. Though we could not converse, Ming Bai, the captain of the riding team, and I had become good friends through our mutual love of the horses that had borne those from another land so generously. I had taken with me, and worn on several days, an American Endurance Ride Conference tee shirt that had a drawing of three mountains on it. The inscription on it read *Three Mountains To Climb—Better Horses, Better Riders, Better Trails,* a theme I thought of for one of the AERC conventions I chaired. Ming Bai was wearing his Mongolian Polo Team shirt. In a totally spontaneous gesture, we both removed our shirts and exchanged them. When I last saw him, he was wearing my AERC shirt and I his Mongolian polo shirt. That was 15 years ago and I still have his shirt. I hope that somewhere in that titanic and fascinating land he still has mine.

Upon our return from the grasslands to the swarming city of Beijing, we had a memorable lunch of French bread, salami and wine in one of the turrets of the Great Wall of China several hours drive from this major city. It was a privately selected area and a fitting conclusion to our trip. There were no other people at the site.

It was raining and we climbed seemingly hundreds of steps to reach the top of the wall. It stretched endlessly in both directions, rising and falling with the undulating terrain. At the time we were there in 1986, we were told that the Great Wall was the only man-made structure that could be seen by our astronauts who circled among the stars we viewed each night. We looked out at the rugged country from the turrets and believed the story that the wall had been breached by invaders who bribed the guards—a menace that no structure, regardless of how formidable, could withstand.

Home seemed faraway and yet, in reality, it was less than a day's travel. Reflecting on our trip, and regretting its termination, we boarded our return flight early the next morning. Our group, with whom we had had eaten, slept, and drunk warm beer from green bottles with so much harmony for several weeks, knew at the airport that we would say "goodbye," go our separate ways and become strangers once again. Or would our shared recollections bond us forever? In our three weeks of communal living, at times under trying circumstances, I do not recall ever hearing an unpleasant word amongst us.

Native Mongolian ponies huddle against the onslaught of a fast approaching storm.

Hungry camel with no place to forage in drought ridden Inner Mongolia—1986.

A Mongolian yurt with the hide of a sheep drying in the sun.

End of the day, Inner Mongolian grasslands—1986.

Mr. Ming Bai wears my AERC tee shirt as I wear his Mongolian Polo Team shirt.

The Great Wall of China 1986.

Americans versus Mongolians share a brisk volleyball game in the village of Jianganne.

Mongolian children watch the American cheerleader at a pick-up volley ball game between Mongolians and Americans—1986.

The funny Americans caused a good deal of giggling among the Mongolian children who had never seen a foreigner before 1986.

EGYPT

As lovers of good horseflesh, mounting Arabian stallions within the shadows of the Sphinx and the Great Pyramids of Giza for a week-long trip into the desert was a boundless thrill. The taxi ride from the Cairo airport to our hotel introduced us to the hustle and bustle of a major city and, as we peered out the cab windows, Bob said, "There they are." "There are what?" I asked. I followed his gaze, and sure enough, there they were—the three great pyramids of Giza. Somehow I had expected a journey into the desert to see them. Finding them right on the edge of town was a surprise. Our hotel was in a perfect location and, by the end of the day, we were walking around these tremendous edifices along with what seemed to be a thousand other tourists mingling with camels, horses, donkeys and hawkers selling their wares. Nothing could detract, or make one feel smaller, than being at the base and looking up the sloping sides of these monuments to Egyptian greatness. How did they do it? Theories abound. Does anyone know for sure? They deserve their rightful place as one of the seven wonders of the world.

We rode in Egypt for five days in the desert and then returned to Cairo by riding along the Nile River. Or rather I did. Bob, turning the tables on me, and for the first time in many years, lay bedridden with the flu. Recovered within a day, but too weak to ride, he stayed at the hotel while I disappeared into the desert without him in the company of an Egyptian tour guide, his two assistants and the only other guest besides me, a gentleman from Germany.

We rode well-mannered, exquisitely beautiful stallions.[3] Alone in the desert with four strangers I had met only hours before, I watched the pyramids diminish in size until they finally disappeared from view. The desert sands presented a bleak landscape and there was little on the horizon ahead except more of the same. It was hard to distinguish where the two, the sand and the horizon, met for one melted into the other with a barely discernible line as it had in Mongolia years before. I felt quite alone in spite of the presence of the others. I was uncomfortable, concerned about Bob and found little solace in the unfamiliar and scowling faces that were my riding companions for the day. Turning back was not an option—there was nothing in any direction. My furtive backward glances saw only the tracks of our horses, the only indication that we had passed this way. Arrangements had been made to pick Bob up later in the day and we were reunited by evening. Alone in our tiny pup tent that was to be our home for the next week, his health was much improved from the night before. We were forced to laugh at the days events as we tried to negotiate by flashlight the sand encrusted stuck zippers of our sleeping bags in a tent in which we could only kneel. As we fell asleep, I told him how much I regretted that he had not been able to share with me the thrill of mounting horses in the shadow of a great pyramid.

Our guide spoke good English, but was unpleasant and drank too much. The distance of our daily rides was pretty much determined by how much imbibing his slight frame tolerated the night before. With Bob now recovered, there was little, however, that could dampen our enthusiasm which easily overshadowed any shortcomings on the part of ride management. We tolerated the strange fare at dinner each night, sitting cross-legged in the guide's tent as he frowned and offered little in the way of hospitality.

Our Arabian stallions were very manageable, loved to run and were elegant, with the refined sculptured heads for which the Egyptian Arabian horse is noted. We galloped up and down sand dune after sand dune and privately chuckled that Rudolf Valentino would have been proud of us. Our guides cared for the horses while we explored pyramids lesser known than the ones near Cairo. We wandered the dirt paths among the date and olive trees of the Fayoum Oasis and escaped a few minor dust storms by retreating to our tent. The ride was essentially a loop and the return trip toward Cairo was along the Nile River. From our horses' backs and between their ears we watched people fishing, washing clothes and watching boats while little children played at the water's edge. Travelers from past centuries must have gazed on much the same scene. The even cadence of our horses' hooves upon the stone roads along the Nile, and under the warm and cloudless Egyptian sky, lulled us and we were totally immersed in our own thoughts of civilizations that shared this same landscape thousands of years before us. We felt dwarfed in time by the ancient wonders of Egypt.

As we drew closer to Cairo, we were once again saddened by the thought that another spirited adventure was nearly at an end. Prior to the riding part of our trip, we had visited the Aswan Dam site and then, in a boat trip down the Nile, marveled (as every traveler in these parts has for centuries) at the wonders of Abu Symbel, the tomb of Ramses II, The Valley of Kings and the Temples at Luxor. I think most young school children's first real interest in other lands is sparked by the stories of the Egyptian pyramids, the Sphinx and King Tut's tomb, mummies and secret passageways. Having seen them first hand, they are just as remarkable as any school child's imagination ever dreamed!

When the riding part of our trip was completed, we toured the Egyptian Agricultural Organization, or EAO, where world-famous Arabian horses are bred and raised. In the paddocks, as many as fifty yearlings raised clouds of dust over our heads as they raced in great circles. The sound of their pounding hooves reverberated throughout the area and you could close your eyes and think of what that sound has meant and the alarm it has evoked throughout history. When man first used the horse as an instrument of war and destruction, approaching hoof beats struck terror into the hearts of villagers who lay in their conquering path.

We culminated our travels with a trip to the Cairo museum to view King Tutankhamen's treasures. The several hours spent there were not nearly long enough and we wished we had planned an extra day to absorb more of it. But, as always, we returned home eager to get back to our family, our own horses and a familiar daily routine.

Our "home" in Egypt for a nine day ride in the desert. Egypt—1989.

Hamming it up for the photographer—Egypt 1989.

Lunch stop. Egyptian Desert—1989.

KENYA

Our memories of riding in Kenya start when we left Nairobi and traveled in Land Rovers down the great Rift Valley and into the Loita Hills. Here our group of twelve Americans first met the horses that were to be our daily companions for the next two weeks. We ranged in age from mid-20s to early 70s, all Americans, and it was immediately apparent that ours would be a congenial group. Selecting our horses the first day, we were mounted and on our way soon thereafter. The growth, lush foliage and tall grasses left no doubt we were in Africa. It was picture postal card perfect. As if to confirm it, and in as dramatic an opening as any movie or play, a herd of about 30 zebras came within our view and then fled at our approach. Most of the herd swerved away from us through the tall grasses, but three apparently wanted a better look at those who would invade their territory. They ran alongside us, frightened, but matching us stride for stride for probably 20 seconds before they crossed in front of us to rejoin their herd. I could not believe my exhilaration. Even though the horse I was on was new to me and was running faster than I would have wished, it really didn't matter. Racing with zebras that first day would have made the trip worthwhile if it had ended right there. It did not, of course, but was merely the preview of the ten days to follow. The ambiance of our trip had been established.

We moved camp everyday. When the sun started to drop in the west, we guided our horses to the new camp location where our tents had been moved, our cots placed inside, and our suitcases and personal belongings carefully arranged. Except for an occasional gallop, the pace was usually leisurely but it was what we wanted. There was abundant wildlife to enthrall and the Masai people to admire—tall, dark and handsome, men and women alike. We were told that a major part of their diet was a drink consisting of blood from their cattle, honey from beehives and urine of their own. We watched amazed as they shot an arrow into the jugular vein of a half grown calf, collected the blood and then squeezed the wound together. As far as I know, the calf survived to give blood another day. With the iron portion of their needs taken care of in this fashion, the honey added the carbohydrate and sugar they needed and the urine provided the salt to round out the diet.

We were invited at one village to be present at a circumcision of a Masai youth early the next day. It is a rite of passage in which the whole community participates and, after which, the young boy, now considered a man, must retreat to the wild and survive on his own to prove his manhood. Bob and I, with a few others in our group, turned the invitation down, but most witnessed the ceremony. The vast chasm between our cultures did not permit our attendance.

Adventure after adventure filled our days, but one in particular was exceptional. Escaping the mid-day sun, we lunched on the banks of the Mara River with our horses tied nearby. A disturbance in the water riveted our attention to one spot. There were probably 30 hippopotamuses in the river or on the sandbar bank, but one was thrashing, climbing out of the water and then agitatedly returning to the river. The explanation for the unusual behavior became obvious. We were witnessing a female in labor. While she was partially immersed, a little head suddenly appeared at her side. She had given birth in the water! What followed could easily vie with any National Geographic nature film for the sheer drama that unfolded before our eyes. With our attention riveted on the scene below, a crocodile, although upstream, apparently sensed the newborn's arrival. It lumbered off the bank, into the water, and headed straight for the infant. Its objective was abundantly clear and we could only stand there, watching and waiting for the the inevitable tragedy about to occur. But there were other eyes on the approaching crocodile as well. A half-grown hippo, already in the water, swam straight toward the approaching invader in an obvious effort to intercept him. They met perhaps fifty feet from the mother and her newborn and, while churned muddy water flew in all directions, the rescuer apparently stomped on the crocodile enough to make it flee underwater as we never saw it again. Our audible sighs of relief were followed by our tour guide's explanation that the rescuer was probably a sibling of the newborn as young hippos stay with the parents through adolescence. The mother, after surviving this trauma, spotted us above her on the bank and turned to face this new threat. We decided she had had enough anxiety for the day and we crept back into the bush and on to our horses for a quick retreat. A final glance showed her floating downstream, small head by her side, and the older sibling nearby.

The trip to Kenya, with the tour group Equitour, was billed as an 'adventure tour' but the accommodations were elegant considering their locations in the jungle. We were presented with roomy tents, warm water with which to wash, respectable outhouses (referred to as 'long drops') and even hot showers. The water, heated over an open fire, was suspended over a tarp-enclosed frame-work masquerading as a shower room. When you pulled a rope, the water fell upon you as if from a sprinkling can. A cocktail hour followed each day's ride and spectacular African sunsets were made more vivid by the libation in hand. Sound effects were courtesy of the monkey population overhead as they leapt from tree to tree, offering us a source of entertainment as wonderful meals were served to weary but fulfilled riders.

My personal highlight of riding in Africa was the giraffe herds. They did not flee at the sight of the horses and riders but rather loped off with eye riveting grace. I do not believe I have ever seen anything as harmonious as running giraffes. Their great bodies flow from side to side with their exquisite necks swaying in perfect rhythm. The elegant long legs unfold and thrust out, almost as if in slow motion, as they extend their stride. The fluidness of their movement is seemingly effortless. I could watch them by the hour, yet had that pleasure only briefly for they fade from view quickly, willowy and silently. Kenya revived thoughts of authors

Beryl Markham and Karen Blixen and their wonderfully descriptive stories of African wildlife. The magic they felt was contagious in just the printed word. Now we were experiencing it as they had, with wide-eyed wonderment and gratitude at the feast Mother Nature provided our searching eyes. We climbed high above the Masai Mara Game Reserve north of the Serengeti to the great escarpment towering over the plains below. We lunched upon the grass where the lions had returned to the grave of Dennis Finch-Hatten in the movie "Out of Africa." Nearby our horses grazed on the verdant growth at their feet, apparently oblivious to the spectacle below them. Far beneath the vista upon which our eyes feasted, lay the great plain where millions of wild animals are born, live and die, hopefully without the knowledge that their days are perhaps numbered by the very species which holds them in so much awe.

Crossing the Mara River Keyna—1988.

Masai children in
Kenya—1988.

"The Pause That Refreshes"
Kenya—1988.

## BOTSWANA

Two years later we once again succumbed to the pull of the
magnificent African continent. I had always thought it was wrong
for tourists to invade the preserves of African wildlife, although I
was guilty. I have since changed my mind. Tourism, if handled

properly, may mean the salvation of the wildlife. Our trip to Botswana proved this to me. Botswana, as with so many other African nations, is a poor country, yet remains one of the last strongholds of wildlife on the African continent. In 1990 we took a horseback safari to find Botswana's emerging economy dependent on exporting beef to the Common Market in Europe. Beef provides the income to feed this country whose population is escalating at a frightening rate. In order to have more grazing land for their cattle, they have encroached further each year upon the feeding grounds of the wildlife. The wild animals are fighting for survival as more and more of them are forced onto less and less open untouched and unspoiled land.

When the people of Botswana see that their wildlife attracts the tourist dollar, one hopes that they will realize that their native wild animals are as valuable a resource as the beef produced by the domesticated cattle.

A fence has been built through a large section of Botswana and, to a certain extent, the wild animals are restricted on one side of the country and the people and the cattle to the other. From the air, one side is overgrazed, brown and drought-ridden. The other is still lush and green, but threatened. The book *Cry of the Kalahari* describes in detail what happened when this fence was erected. The migrating wildebeest, who spent the rainy season in the Kalahari Desert and migrated to the Okavango Delta region in the dry season, ran up against the newly erected fence. They died by the hundreds of thousands. It was an environmental disaster of tragic proportions.

Our horse safari in Botswana brought us into even closer contact with a continent we had found highly hospitable on three previous occasions. We took a 10-year-old grandson, Weston White, the oldest child of our daughter, Barbara, with us. Landing in Harare, the capital city of Zimbabwe, we took a second plane to Victoria Falls and then a third to the town of Maun in the country of Botswana. A fourth flight in a chartered small plane took us deep into the Okavango Delta region, frequently referred to as the Jewel of Africa. On our seven day horse safari, we never saw another person other than each other, our tour guides and the native Africans who cared for the horses and served wonderful meals. The wildlife was abundant and much more wary of us than in Kenya where tourist travel is heavier and the animals more accustomed to people.

Our hosts were P.J. and Barney Bestalink. P.J., a geophysicist, was born in what is now Namibia. When his company asked him to transfer to Australia, he decided against it and, with his wife Barney, the daughter of an English ambassador to Pakistan, decided to stay in Africa and guide horse safaris and run several fish camps. These two, our warmly welcoming hosts, were the perfect companions. In the evenings around the campfire, they shared the secrets they had learned first hand from the animal population they revered.

Our first ride in the veldt, meant to be a calm, cool and collected introduction to our horses, was as memorable as that first ride in Kenya racing with the zebras. Leaving Weston in camp, we rode out with P.J. and Barney. It was just dusk and we were startled upon rounding a thick, wooded corner to find ourselves only a short distance from an immense herd of Cape buffalo. They spotted us immediately. Because they are considered extremely dangerous at close quarters, I was afraid and my instinct was to spur my horse into a rapid retreat. P.J., however, told us to remain still. The buffaloes pawed the ground, charged and the rest remains a blur in my mind except for the cloud of dust, the pounding of many hooves and my nearly as loudly pounding heart. But they stopped short of us. Barney explained that the buffalo have very poor eyesight and seldom charge for more than a couple of hundred yards. As they tried to refocus, and before the dust settled, we guided our horses into the underbrush and out of their range of vision. Having survived, I would not have missed it, but I was glad we had left our grandson in camp.

I very much liked the horse that I had been assigned. Named after a river in Botswana, Linyanti and I proved to be good traveling companions. In his honor, I named the next foal born to Marinera Ranch after him. Although the foal proved to be a filly, it was decided the name was feminine enough to be suitable and she, owned by good friend Nancy Twight, has proved worthy of it.

At night, in our bivouac, we occasionally heard the lions roar as we tried to sleep. We always pitched camp with a river in front of us, and a battery-run electric fence around the back side. Armed guards patrolled at night to assure that the tethered horses (or sleeping guests!) did not become some night prowler's dinner. Because we were the only guests, we enjoyed the luxury of being able to choose when we wanted to ride and for how long. The horses were excellent, our guides, now our good friends, were super companions and we ventured out in all directions by riding both in the mornings and the afternoons, and sometimes in the evenings as well.

Weston, enjoying his first riding experiences, accompanied us on most of our forays out of camp and I hoped his 10-year-old mind would absorb much. I watched with delight his spellbound stare at the sight of dozens of hippopotamuses in a river we were soon to cross on horseback. Elephant herds, giraffe, wildebeest, zebra, impala, lechwe and other wildlife became a daily occurrence in our landscape but never taken for granted. The waters of the Okavango Delta surrounded us and much time was spent sloshing through the wetlands, with camps and lunch breaks on the islands that rose slightly out of the waters. Deep water was crossed guardedly with P.J. leading the way. His rifle and his keen eyesight assured safe crocodile-free passage.

At dusk one day, P.J., Bob and Weston fished and, in a 30-minute period, were able to catch 25 to 30 bream and a type of catfish. Some were thrown back, but enough were saved to be grilled for supper at night. Some evening swims were short lived once it was discovered that leeches[4] shared the slower moving streams with us.

We thoroughly enjoyed the exquisite sunsets as we sat around early evening campfires and the rest of the world seemed very distant. I had a new cam-corder and captured as much of our adventure as I could. When the riding part of our safari was over, P.J. took us by Land Rover to his small private plane to travel to some fish camps. Our transportation had been sitting unattended in an open field for three weeks. I watched with concern as two large tins of gasoline were wedged in behind the seat Weston and I were to occupy. I was not comfortable with the situation. When P.J. grabbed the propeller to give it a quick turn, I secretly hoped the engine would not respond. It disappointed me, however, and sprang to life. The door was held open, and, with my silent apologies to Weston's parents, the two of us climbed into the small space, made even more cramped by the ominous looking gas cans.

Bob and P.J., our horse safari guide turned pilot, were in front of us and while their visibility was much better, I preferred the view of the back of their heads to the view outside. Sensing my apprehension, Bob explained to me that aircraft of this nature could glide to a safe landing if the engine lost power. That might have calmed my fears, but P.J., anxious to show us the wildlife from the air, skimmed the jungle at treetop level. As we approached our fish camp destination, the landing field (somewhat of a misnomer) had some domesticated livestock grazing on it. No problem. We just zipped over them, scarcely clearing their backs. In response they scattered and we landed safely. Clutching Weston's hand, I climbed out of the frightening flying machine and with a deceitful smile, looked at P.J. and said "Oh, that was fun."

Our next five days, though totally different from our horse safari, were equally eye-opening. Exploring the Okavango Delta in flat-bottomed boats, but glancing frequently to the skies to observe the huge flocks of birds, mostly storks, we fished and came closer than one might wish to crocodiles on the banks. At night we went boating again and were startled by the eyes that the flashlight beams picked up. It was often very difficult to tell what lay behind them.

Another departure by private plane deposited us at Chobe National Park where the river banks offered views of great elephant herds bathing and a trip by land rover revealed a pride of lions. A popular tourist area, the Chobe wildlife is much more comfortable being viewed than the animals at the other locations we had visited and, somehow, it was different—not as primal!

One of the fringe benefits of our route to Botswana was the stopover at Victoria Falls. Our first view of this compelling sight was interrupted by the baboons along the walkway overlooking the falls. Much more used to humans than we were to baboons, they were more nonchalant than we as our paths crossed. We spent several days exploring the falls, while thoughts of Humphrey Bogart and Katharine Hepburn drifting toward other falls in *The African Queen* crossed our minds. The falls create a heavy mist and the rainbows cast their colors for close to a mile—an astonishingly beautiful sight. Weston was far braver at peering over the edge than Bob or I, and I again became anxious about returning him safely to his parents. All went well and our long air journey home gave us time to reflect on how privileged we were to have experienced first hand, and in such depth, an Africa that may vanish soon. How I would love to repeat this trip with each of our six grandchildren.

Photo by: PJ Bestalink

Horses and Riders, Okovango Delta, Botswana—1990.

Photo by: Barney Bestalink

Under the Baobob tree in Botswana with grandson, Weston White, 1990.

Bob—Okovango Delta, Botswana, 1990.

Bob and grandson, Weston White, at Victoria Falls, 1990.

BELIZE

Back in the Americas, Belize, formerly British Honduras, beckoned us next. It is a short flight from New Orleans to this Central American country and we had a splendid eight days there enjoying a "turf and surf" program. Our cottage landscaping consisted of an iguana hanging upside down from a sagging branch outside our door, while the calls of native birds at dusk played tag with other less identifiable jungle sounds.

Each day the young American couple who ran the riding tour picked us up and drove to the stables where they kept the horses. Once again, excellent horses, probably the best we have had on any of our trips, introduced us to explorations of wonder. It rained a lot, but it was a warm rain and our flapping slickers kept the horses animated and us dry. Our mounts patiently stood tied to jungle vines as we swam in luscious refreshing pools at the base of waterfalls and as we scrambled up ivy-covered pyramids left from the days when the Mayan culture was dominant. They were there for us when we emerged from deep, dark caves whose farthest recesses our flashlights' beams never reached. Except for one day, we always ate lunch at our horses' feet in the midst of the jungle. The exception was at a movie set left over from the first Indiana Jones picture. In the lagoon type setting, we dog-paddled into a nearby cave while trying to keep our flashlights held out of the water to enable us to see into the darker depths. It was hard work, a bit spooky and we did not stay in the water long.

When we reluctantly bid our horses and our hosts adieu, we boarded a small plane for the 30 mile trip from the capital city of Belize to Ambergis Caye, the location of a barrier reef second only in size to the Great Barrier Reef outside of Cairns that we had visited in Australia. Bob snorkeled and swam and I, once again, true to form, lay in bed with the flu, as I had in South Africa, and cared little about anything.

With these travels, a definite health pattern has developed with me. I seem to always manage to get through the main event nicely in good health. But once the primary feature is over, (or, as Bob says, "when the horses are out of the picture") the stress apparently catches up with me and I come home ailing more frequently than not. Fortunately Bob is tougher and, with the one exception in Egypt, seems to take it all pretty much in stride.

In Belize we tied the horses to jungle vines while we explored caves in which we found broken bits of Mayan pottery.

## OUTER MONGOLIA

Our last adventure tour was in 1995. It was the most physically demanding of them all, perhaps because we had grown older, but it was also the most memorable. We had loved Inner Mongolia, only recently released from Chinese domination when we visited. Now Boojum Expeditions offered a tour to Outer Mongolia, newly freed from Russian jurisdiction.

Our seemingly endless flight from Los Angeles across the Pacific to the scurrying rush of Beijing was uneventful. Going into the interior of Asia was another story. We flew to Ulan Bator, the capital of Outer Mongolia. Arriving in town almost simultaneously with the Dalai Lama, we rushed to the town square for the speech he was to give that we knew we would not understand, but nevertheless could not afford to miss. A sudden thunder shower sent us hastening for shelter along with hundreds of Mongolians who had come to hear their spiritual leader. Pushed and shoved by the crowd, we emerged back into the open to find that Bob's wallet was missing from his back pocket. To be stranded in Outer Mongolia without his 250 American dollars (a year's salary for a Mongolian), traveler's checks and credit cards left him feeling vulnerable. Unable to do a thing about it, we decided it would be hard to use American plastic in Outer Mongolia so made no effort to even report the loss of the Master Card. The cash would never be retrieved and I still had traveler's checks. Where we were headed, there would be no need for any of the lost items anyway.

One of our fellow travelers, with much forethought, put all her valuables in a fanny pack around her waist. Her efforts at safekeeping also proved to be in vain. When she emerged from the same shelter we had sought, her pack had been slit (apparently with a razor) and the contents removed. I really do not think the Mongolians as a nation should be tainted by these two experiences. The crowd was large, and the fair-skinned and taller Americans stood out and were obviously targeted by some dishonest persons. We met so many that we would trust with everything we hold dear that we were not soured by the shortcomings of a few.

From Ulan Bator we took a somewhat ancient prop-driven plane to the town of Moron where we climbed aboard an old Russian troop truck. Perched on wooden benches lined up on each side of the bed of the truck with our luggage in between, fourteen of us drove for two and a half days over primarily roadless terrain to the interior where we met our horses and our Mongolian guides. It was a rough ride and we were happy to discover in the next few days that our horses were far more comfortable to be aboard than the troop truck.

There were nine North American guests on this trip and there never was a more diverse group. We consisted of two Canadian women (one a museum curator and the other a geologist), a Chinese hairdresser from San Francisco, a woman tugboat operator from San Francisco Bay, a luthier (one who manufactures stringed instruments) from Ann Arbor, Michigan, and a young, recently married couple, both attending veterinarian school in Colorado. Bob and I, as usual, were the oldest. We were a motley crew but all were prepared mentally for whatever new experiences the following days wished to send our way.

It is not possible to convey to others our adventures of the following week with trite phrases. We were totally isolated from the outside world. Telephone or radio communications were nonexistent; we were three days' arduous travel from a paved road with no protection from weather other than our small tents. We had to put our faith for survival in the hands of the friendly Mongolians and in the small horses we were riding that also packed our supplies.

Most of our days were spent crossing open country of rolling hillsides. Bob and I always rode together and our two horses were as compatible as we. Our meals were not the Four Season variety. They were better. We were usually hungry, and frequently cold and wet, so the huge jars of Skippy's peanut butter and loaves of bread were consumed rapidly. The chocolate bars for dessert rounded out a typical noontime meal. Who could ask for anything more? I never had a meal on that trip that I did not happily anticipate and relish as it slipped down my throat. Exercise and hunger do wonderful things for the palate.

We were told to give our individual horses a name of our choosing. I promptly christened mine "Bon Ami" and hoped that is how I would consider him at the end of our journey. Our mounts were sturdy, strong, long-suffering and sure-footed. Our confidence rose in these animals as surely as the daily clouds, which never failed to seek us out for a good drenching.

Our most arduous day took us over a 10,000-foot pass in rain and sleet. Bent and leaning into the storm, Bob pointed to the path ahead. Two men, mounted on fast-moving reindeer, had joined our group. I speculated as to whether they were in as much wonder of us as we were of them. Our single file ascent on the tortuous rock strewn trail was gradual, but enough to shift the burden on one overloaded pack horse. His rebellious gyrations achieved his purpose of divesting himself of the unwanted load upon his back and we watched in horror as our sleeping bags, personal items and jars of Skippy's peanut butter were scattered on the wet and windswept slope. The errant beast 's freedom was of short duration. He was quickly retrieved as the wranglers went about the miserable task of gathering up the far flung items and returning them to the back of the recalcitrant animal.

Crossing the summit of the craggy pass with the leaden skies above, it was easy to think of more hospitable locations than our present one, but our sense of adventure never flagged. Continuing down the northern slope, we arrived within several miles of the Siberian border at the camp of the reindeer people. It had stopped raining, but I was cold and beginning to shiver. Suffering from the early stages of hypothermia as I slid off my horse, I was taken by these friendly people into a smoke filled tent and, while sitting cross legged on a reindeer hide, was handed a bowl of hot reindeer milk. I drank it eagerly for the warmth alone. Trying to show my appreciation, I smiled, smacked my lips and rubbed my stomach to let them know how much I appreciated their hospitality. They smiled back and graciously offered me a second bowl. Not wanting to appear rude, I accepted it. Nausea was almost immediate and I realized their offering was as rich as melted butter, and, though now warm, I had traded one discomfort for another. I crept into the small tent Bob had pitched on the tundra and could not have been more miserable for the rest of a seemingly endless day. I managed to crawl out briefly to sit on a reindeer for picture taking and to be reminded of what a valuable animal they are to these people. Their lives are entirely dependent upon the reindeer—food, clothing, shelter and transportation. We were there in their summer time. I do not see how they survive a winter, although they do migrate down into the larch forests where the winds blowing out of Siberia are a little less severe.

When we started our journey the next day for the return trip, I once again turned in the saddle and looked back. Instead of the lonely farmer who had given us shelter in Inner Mongolia years before, there were men, women and children watching us disappear up the rock strewn pass we had crossed in the rain the day before. I raised my hand and the signal of farewell was returned. The sun shone weakly now and we descended single file the treacherous rocky trail leading into the larch forests. The creeks we had crossed easily yesterday were now swollen, raging torrents from the storm that had assaulted us as errant travelers on our way to the reindeer camp. Ford after ford was tried and I marveled at the guides' horses who were so obedient they stepped into the turbulent waters without hesitation. But, each time they turned back and we knew that the crossing was considered too risky. Further downstream, a suitable spot for an attempt was found. The river was somewhat wider here and a bit more shallow so the horses would be less apt to be swept off of their feet. The first Mongolian to cross reached the opposite bank and with a smile indicated that we should follow. We did, but not without some hesitation and holding of breath. If a horse had lost its footing in the torrent, I do not think either it or the rider would have survived. As Bon Ami and I approached the step down into the swirling waters, I nudged his ribs with my heels and said out loud "You *can* do this!" He was as resolved as I was to get to the other side safely and his feet found purchase among the rocks and boulders and we emerged on the other side wet but victorious. We were among the first to cross and the sense of helplessness as I watched others tackle the angry waters kept me taut and alarmed. Bob's horse, a little taller than the others, handled the crossing nicely to my great relief. Some horses floundered badly, but somehow managed to stay upright and reach the opposite bank. As it was, Alice, the geologist from Canada, had her horse sink and flounder in a bog in another area. While Alice recovered from her mud bath, her camera was not as lucky and its days of recording our journey were gone forever.

Another exhilarating day occurred when we crossed a rather wide but fast moving muddy river on a raft that might have been built by Tom Sawyer. Four or five seriously reluctant horses at a time were loaded on it along with their riders, now on foot. The horses had never been water borne before and it took a good bit of persuasion applied to their rear ends to get them on board. Uncomfortable in this situation, they huddled together miserably on one side with equally apprehensive humans on the other side holding on to the reins to keep them from sliding off. The result was a totally unstable raft with one end submerged a couple of feet in the water by the weight of the horses. The other side protruded several feet in the air, with the turbulent waters threatening to tip over the whole ill conceived undertaking at any moment. A hand pull cable was strung across the river about five feet above the water and the Mongolian boatman hauled on the cable, hand over hand, as we headed for the far bank. Had he released his grip even briefly, we would have floated down river with little guarantee of a safe landing. When we reached the other side, there was no dock. The horses and people jumped off simultaneously and scrambled up the slippery mud bank. With each departure, the raft jolted and heaved and threatened the balance of those of us still waiting for our chance to leap for shore. Muddy wet feet and legs were proof that we jumped neither high nor far enough when it was our turn. The boatman, I am told, received 4 cents per horse and 2 cents per person for his troubles. Once safely on the other side, I would have gladly emptied my wallet in gratitude of safe passage if asked. But neither would I trade the unexpected adventure for any amount of gold. It was an astounding experience.

More adventures followed, but the memories that linger longest are those of gallant little horses and the Mongolian people who unfailingly met us with smiles and hospitality. As a traveler, I fall short in many departments. I do not have the interest I should in the politics and religions of the countries we visit, but leave that up to Bob. I love seeing the different countrysides, the flora and fauna, and I especially enjoy the one-to-one personal exchange with the people. The mothers and the children in simple farm hovels have my sympathy and my love, neither of which they necessarily need. Smiling faces were evidence of a contentment not often found in more developed countries. I found that the marked differences separating our very diverse cultures could be breached by the simple gesture of admiring a baby held in the arms of a loving Mongolian mother.

My fondest memories of all of our trips are of the horses and my undiminished zest to be ten feet tall as I see the panorama of the world unfold between their ears. I have always returned with horseshoes, bits of assorted tack and on one occasion, a wildebeest skull which hangs over my barn. I picked it up while riding in Kenya and it had to be boiled in Africa for an hour before I could bring it into this country. I carried it onto the plane in a burlap sack, tucked it under my seat and was thankful no one ever asked me what the sack contained. Passing through airport security did not so much as cause a raised eyebrow.

In Outer Mongolia, at Lake Hovsgal, I found a bleached yak skull which also came home with me to join that of the wildebeest on my barn. Before I left Mongolia, I tried to give it to a Mongolian

Struggling to get on the raft. Outer Mongolia—1995.

Struggling to get off of the raft in Outer Mongolia.

truck driver while explaining to him through an interpreter that all rich Texans had steer skulls or horns on the radiators of their Cadillacs and I felt that it should adorn his truck. His interpreted reply was that he was not a rich Texan so it would be wrong.

Interestingly enough, I have only had one person ever inquire about my barn decorations. I guess it is assumed they are just good old American steer skulls. Or maybe they fear a a long discourse on their origin if they ask. They are constant reminders to me of memories that I cannot forget, yet have difficulty in describing to others. The "D" in creative writing at Stanford University continues to haunt me. Creative riding seems to be more my style!

I would like to end this chapter on rides of exploration by saying we have felt physically and personally safe on all of these trips except on our second trip to Mongolia, where we did have some fleeting moments when we questioned our judgment and vowed never to leave home again. At times I have had some apprehension about the horses and the gear. I have found that I underplay my riding experience when asked if I have ridden very much. If I say I have horses of my own, it is immediately assumed that I am an expert and I will then most likely be given one of the more obstreperous animals whose training leaves a lot to be desired. Whenever I have expressed apprehension, the tour leaders have been gracious and understanding. Their livelihood depends on our dollars and, with the exception of our leader in Egypt, they do make a real and successful effort to please.

People have asked me if I could go back to one of these places, which would I choose. It would either be Botswana for the wild animals or Outer Mongolia for the adventure. Although the landscapes, the people, the cultures are completely different, the feeling of being totally removed from civilization as we know it in our day-to-day lives wins out. It is usually a reflective time. There are no background noises, no jet planes overhead, no freeway noises, no radios or TVs. No amenities. No help if needed. These times are the closest I have ever come to being a "deep thinker," especially at night when the stars are at their brightest and the sky does not end. Reality returns quickly when I arrive home and the adventures become more like a dream and I wonder if they truly happened. When I look at my barn with my wildebeest and yak skulls, I know they did.

Home—Outer Mongolia.

Bob and friendly reindeer, Outer Mongolia—1995.

A proud Outer Mongolian with his horse.

Happy Campers—Outer Mongolia, 1995.

CHAPTER THIRTEEN

# Multi-day and International Rides

*Love horses, care for them;*
*Only in them lie honor and beauty.*

Verses by the sage Ben-Sassa

In the early 1980s a new concept was introduced to the endurance world, multi-day rides. These rides certainly had their vehement opponents, but those in favor successfully argued that the true test of endurance was the ability of a horse to continue day after day. I knew it was possible from my South African three-day ride, but the new proposal encompassed a 250-mile trail to be ridden in segments of 50 miles a day for five days. The rider would have the choice of doing the entire course on one horse or changing horses as he wished. Five-day rides of 50 miles each day? It seemed excessive. A veterinarian by the name of Dave Nicholson presented the concept to the American Endurance Ride Conference, and it met with great resistance and near fisticuffs. He finally received AERC approval and staged his first five-day 250-mile ride on part of the original Pony Express Trail. He proved his point. It was indeed possible to have a horse carry a rider for five successive days on demanding trails of 50 miles or more and finish with an animal sound of wind and limb.

Because of Dr. Nicholson's persistence, many of us have seen our country as it appeared to the pioneers, to the Pony Express Riders, Lewis and Clark, Butch Cassidy and the Sundance Kid, General Pershing and Pancho Villa, and now, as it appears to late 20th century riders. With an irresistible penchant for adventure, Bob and I have participated in approximately 30 of these multi-day rides. From our horses' backs we have seen 750 miles of the original Pony Express Trail beginning in Fairfield, Utah and on to Carson City, Nevada. From that point we have crossed the mountains and joined the Tevis Cup trail for a hundred miles and then continued on to Sacramento, California. We have walked in the steps of pioneers and marveled at the courage of these people

Bob Suhr and HCC Gazal+/ at the finish line of the 5 day 265 mile Death Valley Ride in 1986.

Photo by: Ellen Waddell

who came west under conditions of hardship with which we cannot possibly identify. We have paused at the abandoned Pony Express stations and reflected upon the bravery of the teenage riders who ventured into Indian territory, their ladened saddle bags filled with precious mail. History books tell us that the average age of a rider was 16 and that orphans were preferred.

We have ridden the Mexican border from El Paso, Texas to Shakespeare, New Mexico in the area where Pancho Villa and General Pershing faced off. We have traveled the Applegate Lassen Trail from the Humboldt River near Winnemucca, Nevada to the California border and camped at the same locations as those who came in covered wagons a century and a half before us. From the backs of our horses we have surveyed landmarks first noted in mid-19th century journals, carefully inscribed by men who did not know, as we modern day riders do, what lay beyond the next mountain range. The diaries of the brave souls of the wagon trains recorded points of interest faithfully. Further south we traveled the canyons of Bryce and Zion National Parks with the red cliffs towering above us, challenging our sure-footed horses to carry us to the tops. We have explored Death Valley National Monument below sea level where the 20 Mule Teams pulled the Borax wagons across a stunningly austere landscape. By the end of the same day we have risen to the 6,000 foot level and looked down upon our lost footprints, now covered by the shifting desert sands.

Due to the enormously popular Race of Champions, which gave us "pomp and circumstance" such as the sport had never seen before, our horses have climbed the slopes of Colorado's Pike's Peak and mingled with the elk herds of Wyoming and Montana. We have ridden in the Dakotas, almost within the shadow of Mount Rushmore. Together we have fanned out from the Black Rock Desert, Soldier Meadows and Mud Lake to see our West from high plateaus and from the depths of deep canyons where the wild horses still run. It is impossible to become complacent on these rides. The utter insecurity of what tomorrow may bring is

Riders on the 5 Day 250 Mile Pony Express Trail in Utah in 1986.

coupled with an earnest anticipation of what will occur. Trail Blazer Magazine published my article about one multi-day ride in which Bob and I participated. The essence of our sport, from my perspective, was in full view on this particular ride.

## THIS WAS SOLDIER MEADOWS

In recent years the concept of multi-day rides has spread. It was truly exemplified in the recent Soldier Meadows 250 mile five day ride in the northwestern corner of Nevada. It took forever to get there with a pick-up pulling a horse trailer. The last forty miles were two hours long—two hours of dust, washboard dirt roads and more dried up sage brush than you need to see in a lifetime. But fifty riders, with perhaps seventy horses, figured it worth the time and effort. They were richly rewarded.

Endurance Riding reaches its ultimate height when all segments of our population are represented in one ride. Endurance riding is winning, crossing the finish line first, getting the biggest trophy. Endurance riding is finishing last with a horse in great shape. Endurance riding is starting the ride and being pulled. Endurance riding is seeing country you never would have had the good fortune to witness if some hard working ride manager hadn't put it all together for you. Endurance riding is young and old and in between all striving for the same goal—to cross a certain area of this great land within a certain number of hours. Endurance riding is accepting failure graciously on one day because you know there will be triumphs on other days. It is good fellowship on the trail and in the camp. But perhaps more importantly, endurance riding is bridging the gap between humankind and the animal kingdom, which we hopefully do not exploit in our search for our own personal highs.

Soldier Meadows was five days of misery, dust, rocks, heat and wind. Five days of glory—good people, good horses, exquisite trails and the privilege of being on top of the world. The West as in Lonesome Dove and the stories of Will James and Zane Grey. The West as in our heritage.

Soldier Meadows was listening to our horses respond to the wild ones' nickers, the instant raising of the halter restricted heads, the expression in the eyes of our saddle marked horses as some deep longing was stirred in their depths at the sight of the dust cloud left by horses who have never felt cold steel in their mouths or a rider upon their back. Freedom, perhaps. The mind dwells on how long they would survive if we turned them loose to join the wild herd.

Soldier Meadows was Mae Schlegel at age seventy-nine and her twenty four year old horse riding one hundred miles in two days—climbing four thousand feet above the valley floor and thrilling as a young child at the sight of the wild horses five hundred feet above us. But if you ride with Mae you have to listen to her complain. "Darn horse, pulling my arms right out of the sockets. What am I going to do about him? Tried to buck me off at Castle Rock." Darn horse, right. She had loved and cared for him from his first breath and she would continue to care for him until his last.

Endurance riding. Soldier Meadows was watching Tom Bowling and his kids saddle up in the morning to start the day's adventures. Holly and Shawn learned what it meant to be hot and tired and dirty. They also learned what it was to sing songs while trying to find the trail through Little High Rock Canyon where the golden cliffs narrow and bogs await those not paying attention to their horses' path. They learned what it was to set a day's goal and achieve it by day's end in the form of the finish line back at camp. What rich memories for their adult years this one caring and giving man has furnished them. Endurance Riding.

Soldier Meadows was Lavone Booth and her crew of Roxy, Carol, Dean, Barbara and the young Ohioans, Adam and Ryan. It was Lavone and her blue and white truck and her gallons of iced lemon tea and her inevitable question as you dismounted at the noon vet check. "Do you want turkey, ham or tuna with mayonnaise or mustard? Here's a chair. The water for your horse is over there. Do you need hay?" It was the young efficient veterinarian, Rod Meier, who, with fifty horses spread out over the remotest area in the continental United States, managed to keep track of each and every one at all times. I can't figure it out. He never seemed to rush, but you never had to wait. Ride Management—under appreciated, under paid, long suffering and long on patience. Without them we would be sitting at home instead of in the saddle.

Soldier Meadows was sixty-seven year old, six thousand miler Bob Walz going five days on his fifteen year old nearly six thousand mile horse he had been riding steadily for ten years. The fly-by-nights should take a lesson from these two companions who, by the way, took home the Best Condition trophy—a richly deserved honor.

Soldier Meadows was people packing up and leaving after a couple of days when either they or their horses had had enough; it was people sitting in camp a week just so they could be of help to a friend or spouse at day's start or end. It was watching the wild horses come down to the lake at night to drink. What a feast we must have left them in spilled grain and left over hay when we pulled out of camp and returned their last stronghold to them.

Soldier Meadows was a western band and barbecued steaks the last night under a starry sky. It was the hot shoes Roger, Penny, and Arlene winning; it was the young man Trevor, swallowing his disappointment at being pulled the last day, helping with the barbecue; it was the solid gold five horses who managed to go all five days and come in running the last day—Rashina, Brusally Skoraik, Ambers Folio, Tommy and Rushcreek Option.

Soldier Meadows was the man from Down Under, Australian Jack Boswell, riding Andy Bender's young stallion and fitting in so well because Endurance Riding knows no boundaries. It was flat tires, no lights and rebelling engines. It was the massaging waters of the hot springs and the yip of coyotes in the night. It was electrolytes and iced legs, fly spray and the sound of a farrier's hammer. How many horseshoes were left in those miserable rocks? It was the sky that went on without end, the Black Rock Desert from 8,500 feet, the occasional cluster of green trees signifying a nearby stream, the old ranch houses, the herds of antelope and the brilliant wild flowers.

Endurance Riding. Where your successes feed your ego and you learn from your failures. Endurance Riding. The great leveler of young and old, rich and poor. Endurance Riding which at its best should perhaps seize from the past a new motto—"*One for All and All for One.*" This WAS Soldier Meadows. This IS Endurance Riding.

At the same time that multi-day rides were becoming fairly well established as an integral part of the endurance world, the sport was becoming truly international. Australia was the second country to adopt the concept of riding a horse a hundred miles in one day. Many more countries quickly followed. Endurance riding is now a recognized sport in over 60 countries. It naturally followed that international competition would be the next step. In 1986, American horses were flown to Rome for the first International 100-Mile One-Day Endurance Ride. In the 1988 World Championship Ride, my horse and I flew to Virginia as one of the ten rider/horse teams to represent the United States on a difficult trail that had us fording the Shenandoah River in early dawn and again in the dark of midnight. Since that time, world championship competitions have been held in Sweden, Spain, Holland, France and the Arab Emirate State of Dubai. Endurance enthusiasts would like to see endurance riding become an Olympic sport and many persons view the possibility with optimism. One won-

Photo Credit: © 1988 Genie Stewart-Spears

HCC Rusghala at the World Championship Endurance Ride in Virginia in 1988.

ders if Wendell Robie, when he made that first 100-mile one-day ride in 1955, envisioned Olympic gold. Or did his horizon extend no farther than the gold of the setting sun over the Auburn hills where it all began?

CHAPTER FOURTEEN

# HCC Gazal +/

*And when the dust settled*
*And his trumpeting left the air*
*Silent hoof prints bore testimony*
*A monarch had passed.*

j.s.

I have always felt that it takes just one special horse to put a rider on the endurance map. Many times these special horses are not chosen by the discriminating eye of a knowledgeable horseman who sees the proper conformation, the special look in the eye or the extra fluidness of motion, but rather by happenstance or pure luck. Then, if the ability of the horse is recognized and handled properly, the two, horse and rider, become well known on the endurance circuit. In 1980 Bob and I needed a horse. A friend, Jim Remillard, told us about a young gelding he thought would suit our purposes. The horse had no endurance record, but he came from the Hyannis Cattle Company in Nebraska and their horses had proven themselves repeatedly on the endurance trail.

We did not ride HCC Gazal +/ [1] before purchasing him. The look in this horse's eye and Jim's recommendation were all that was needed to make a decision.

Gazal's excellence was apparent to me the first time I rode him in a limited distance ride. Bob had ridden him on two limited-distance 25-milers. I took him on his third. It was a 25-mile battle between the power of his legs on the ground and the strength of my hands on the reins. That day he won the Best Condition Award, a prelude of things to come. I wrote his breeder the next evening and said, "I have found my Haggin Cup[2] horse. Give me two years and he will win it." He did, and then, he won it twice more. He put my name on the endurance map rather than vice versa.

HCC Gazal +/ en route to the Race of Champions in Colorado where he won the Best Condition Award—a trip for two on the QE II to England.

HCC Gazal +/ and Bob Suhr at the Nye Ranch Ride in 1988 where they won the Best Condition Award.

Gazal was a proud horse, blessed with desire. A tremendous athlete, there was only one way to ride a horse such as this one in an endurance race and that was for the top. Gazal won rides for either Bob or me at 50 miles, at 100 miles and at 250-mile multi-day rides. Seven times he carried me down that Tevis Cup trail and seven times he brought me home with another silver buckle. The 17,000 feet of ascent and 22,000 feet of descent in that rugged 100 miles never conquered him. I don't think he really ever took a deep breath—he was born a cut above the rest. He honored me with three Haggin Cup wins, an award presented to the rider of the horse judged to be in the best condition of the first ten horses to cross the finish line after 100 miles of the Tevis Cup trail. Years later I shudder at the memories of some of those rides. Gazal was never a runaway but he could be head-strong. He had a tender mouth and I never worried about being able to stop him, but he liked to go sideways; he liked to whinny at the other horses; he was just alive with joie de vivre. I thrilled to him, and the ardour and the keenness with which he coursed over that Sierra Nevada hundred mile trail from east to west were high points of my riding career.

Gazal had a chance to win the Tevis Cup in 1986. With an entry list of 270 riders, he had managed, with comparative ease, to stay close to the lead horses most of the day. By the time we reached the American River crossing, we had neatly put about 83 miles of our goal of 100 miles behind us. We were closely bunched with four other riders, some of whose horses still looked fresh, but a couple of them had begun to show the effects of a long day on the trail. Gazal was quick to attack the river crossing, thrusting his mouth into the belly deep water for long gulps, but never slowing his forward motion. The rushing waters of the American River were invigorating to him and he emerged on to the familiar trail on the other side refreshed and eager to run. He was never an easy horse to ride as his great strides threw the rider further out of the saddle than most horses do. I never felt as though I rode him well and nearly 85 miles had taken their toll on me but not Gazal. The narrow trails on which we had spent most of the day had now broadened into a dirt road, undulating and curving with each turn in the river it paralleled. He galloped and with each thrusting stride, I became more physically weary than I had ever been on a ride. I grabbed his mane with a hand on each side of his handsome neck and had to work to maintain my balance. A half mile from the last vet check, 6 miles from the finish line, we caught the leading horse and rider, a good friend of mine. The first one to leave this checkpoint would be the horse that recovered to the 64 beats per minute pulse requirement in the shortest time. I knew then that the opportunity to win the Tevis Cup was within my reach. I don't think I ever truly considered myself that good a rider until that moment nor did I ever have illusions until then of being the first to finish.

I knew instinctively when I could take Gazal to the veterinarians without risking the 10 minute penalty that would be assessed against me if I presented him before his pulse had dropped. It was risky, but I took him before any of the other five riders who also must have realized that this would be a horse race to the finish. Gazal's eyes told me that he was not stressed. The veterinarian cleared us and I knew that we would be the first to embark on the last six mile stretch. Leading the next riders to leave by two minutes, we had plenty of daylight ahead to show us the way. The wide road was left behind and the two mile trail to No Hands Bridge was narrow and precarious. Gazal swung his head in frustration when I would not release the tight grip I had on the reins. He was totally familiar with the trail and was well aware that the feed bucket was just down the road a few miles. But, I simply did not have the strength in reserve to turn him free. Exhausted by the many miles since dawn, I did not believe I could maintain my balance upon his back. Once running, I doubted that I any longer had the strength to control him. I knew the trail ahead was treacherous for the next couple of miles. One horse wide with long drop-offs, I sadly moved aside at a rare wide spot to let two horses that had caught us pass. Gazal became more frustrated as they pulled away from us and even more difficult to handle. The riders that had overtaken us were friends and, while it bothered me to be passed, I knew I would finish in time to have a chance at a third Haggin Cup. We started across the bridge as the sun was setting beyond the Auburn hills, and friends at the crossing were aware I had lost my lead and I somehow felt that I had let them down. We finished in third place. I believe that I had the top horse that day. He did not have the top rider. Endurance riding is a team effort— one horse, one rider—the best combination wins.

But Gazal was not to be denied the next morning. At the Best

Condition judging he put on a thrilling performance. He pranced, he danced and entranced. And he won his third Haggin Cup, a record that still stands. I held a Haggin Cup record now, but I still had one more goal. I now, in 1990, stood on the brink of becoming the first person to ever earn a 20 Day—2000 Mile buckle. It took me 25 years to reach this point. Ride statistics show that an average of 50 percent of the starters reach the finish line in this race. I wanted to ride conservatively in order to increase my chances of finding Auburn. I would not be riding the last few miles at dusk as I had previously, but at the slower pace, and it would be dark. I now had finished 11 straight Tevis Cup Rides without being pulled. I knew the law of averages said I was long overdue for a disqualification. I also knew it would be hard to restrain Gazal. As the date approached, my apprehension mushroomed.

I figured I would be riding the most important ride of my life as I reached for the first-ever 2000 mile Tevis Cup silver buckle. I worked earnestly on my conditioning and training program. I wanted Gazal to be perfect for what I expected to be my final ride down this trail at which I hoped to reach my long term goal. It was not to be! Five weeks before the big day, he fell at a gallop with me during a training ride. With great 'loyalty,' he left me lying on the ground in a pitiful heap while he romped home. I was reminded of the saying that *'there are two kinds of riders—those that have gone off and those that are going to go off.'* I silently wished that I had not found it necessary to prove it quite so many times over the course of my riding career. (Remember, it had all started with Andy on Thanksgiving Day. Fifty-eight years later the pattern continued!) I watched Gazal disappear on the sharp up hill trail with his head high and his tail flagged and I was thankful that he had not been injured. I was not so sure about myself.

When I tried to get up on my feet, sharp abdominal pains warned me to not try to rise again. Fortunately, Bob was in the yard. The riderless horse racing up the driveway sounded the alarm. He soon found me not far down the trail and for the first time felt the necessity to call 911. The fire department arrived and the litter was held at each corner by strong young men who carried me to the top of the hill to the waiting paramedics who would transport me to the emergency ward. By the time we arrived, I was sitting up, and the unexplained sharp stomach pains had disappeared. But I could not lift my left arm and, as the nurse cut my tee shirt off my body, she announced that, "why, of course, you have broken your collarbone. It will be fine in a couple of months." A couple of months!!! Didn't she know the Tevis Cup Ride was in five weeks? What on earth could she be thinking?!!

Returning home several hours later, my right arm banded closely to my body by a sling, my mood was less than joyous. I had little time to heal before the ride and would not be able to train during that period. Unhurt by the fall, I knew Gazal would be too strong for me to handle with a healing broken bone even if my recovery was rapid. I was heartbroken and defeated.

Rescue came in the form of a gentle little mare offered by a friend, Maryben Stover. Her short bay horse had the funny name of Rushcreek Q-Ball, crooked legs and a crooked white blaze running down her face. Maryben said she was smooth as glass and could be controlled easily with just a halter. That was what I needed. Q-Ball had never done a 100-mile ride, but she was a fast trotter and, besides, I did not have many choices. Maryben's offer was quickly accepted and, though I had not been on a horse in five weeks, I began that last journey over the Sierra Nevada. It was a ride filled with nostalgia for I truly believed that, if successful, I would never attempt to conquer that trail again. Q-Ball did her job, willingly gliding down the trail quite effortlessly as though this was what she had in mind all along. I humbly received my 2000 Mile 20 Days Tevis Cup buckle that Maryben and Rushcreek Q-Ball made possible. It was identical to that first one earned 26 years before except for the wording and the rubies on each side of the running horse. I had Q-Ball's name engraved on the back so that I would never forget the little bay mare with the funny name and the crooked legs. The collarbone that ached the day before the ride and the day after never bothered me on Tevis Cup day. Under the spell of the Indian Riding Moon, the adrenaline flowed and the endorphins did their job. I now had a string of 12 successive finishes.

My goal had been achieved and I should have been happy, but knowing I would never traverse those golden mountains again on the back of a horse made me nostalgic. While it was my decision alone to stop at twenty completions, and I knew Bob was relieved, it was a bittersweet time. As Q-Ball carried me that last meditative mile to the finish line, I was afraid it might be the last time I felt ten feet tall. God had blessed me so many times with good horses that I doubted there could be any more in my future. I returned Q-Ball to Maryben and, forgiving Gazal for his momentary lapse in sure-footedness, continued to ride other endurance trails on him.

Gazal was campaigned in endurance competition for ten years and eight thousand miles. My decision to retire him proved that I still had some self-preservation instincts. He had fallen twice with me and both times I made excuses that exonerated him. The third time he went down, I made a pact with God en route to the ground that if He let me survive this fall, I would never ride Gazal again. I survived and I kept my pact. Gazal was 16 years old at the time of the last fall. At age 25, he lives a life of retirement and privilege at Marinera Ranch and our love, pride and respect for him is as great as when he was achieving fame.

Gazal is the most generous horse I have ever known and he willingly shared his excellence with whoever chose to ride him on a particular day. He never held a grudge and mistakes made by his riders were always forgiven in the next stride. He was nobility from the day he was born and, though his dynamic vigor is now compromised by age, he continues to stand just a little taller than the others. Gazal's record speaks of his worthiness. And, he is still the prettiest horse that ever went down the Tevis Cup trail.

Todd Nelson, DVM presents the Haggin Cup to Julie Suhr for Gazal's second Best Condition win in 1984.

HCC GAZAL+/ Competed for 10 years 1980–1990
    Ridden by Bob or Julie Suhr
Total of 7,932 AERC miles plus two unsanctioned Tevis Cup
    Rides and one unsanctioned Race of Champions.
Completed 144 out of 148 rides.
Received First Place and Best Condition Awards at 50, 100
    and 250 miles.
Completed 17 multi-day rides of 250 or more miles—a
    record at one time.
Winner of three Haggin Cups—1983, 1984, 1986—a record.
Completed seven consecutive Tevis Cup Rides.
California State Lightweight Endurance Champion, 1984
Endurance Horse Registry of America—Legion of Merit,
    1984
Endurance Horse Registry of America—Hall of Fame, 1985

International Arabian Horse Association—Legion of Merit, 1985

International Arabian Horse Association—Region II Lightweight Champion, 1985

International Arabian Horse Association—Region II Best Condition Champion, 1985

Winner of the Race of Champions Best Condition Award, 1985

Winner of the Race of Champions West Region Championship, 1985

International Arabian Horse Association Legion of Supreme Honor, 1986

Winner 250-Mile Pony Express Fastest Time, 1986

Winner 250-Mile Pony Express Best Condition, 1986

AERC West Region Best Condition Champion, 1986

California State Horsemen's Association Best Condition Award, 1986

Winner 265-Mile New Mexico Renegade Fastest Time, 1988

Winner 265-Mile New Mexico Renegade Mile Best Condition, 1988

Inducted into the AERC Hall of Fame, 1989

### In Honor of Gazal+/

*His hooves have traced the steps of the fleet Pony Express
ponies. He has climbed the paths of the Bitterroot Range to
cavort in the alpine meadows of the high country of Wyoming.
The trail of Pancho Villa along the Mexican border has had
his shadow cast upon it. He has raced with the best within
the spell of Pike's Peak. He has pricked his ears at the
crashing of the Pacific surf as he has woven his way through
the dark redwood forests of his California home. Seven times
he has looked to the West before
dawn and heroically propelled his great body a hundred
miles down a trail meant to challenge all comers. He has*

*fought against the restraint of hard steel in his tender
mouth—his excellence inhibited by a less than brave rider.
He has watched the sun rise at ten thousand feet and set below
sea level when he responded to a rider's need for adventure.
He has wrung his great neck with impatience and the
vitality from within. He has bellowed his displeasure when
separated from a treasured stablemate. His nickers have
greeted those who love him most at the early morning slam of
a back door that means another day, and, more importantly,
another meal.
He has watched the moon rise over a dry lake bed as the
peace and quiet of an endurance camp in late evening descend
upon both man and beast. What primitive stirrings are
invoked within by the silhouettes of wild horses running free
across a Nevada skyline? He has tucked his head low as he
faced into a wind-driven snowstorm and he has quenched his
thirst eagerly on the hottest of summer days.
His smooth bay flanks have never failed to respond to the
nudge of a rider's heel. He has stood patiently confined in the
tight constraints of a trailer while his nostrils and lungs
were assailed by the emissions blanketing the ribbons of
asphalt that invariably led to one more test of his excellence.
His home is not just a fenced corral, but also in the hearts
of those who love him. For ten years he performed in the
most demanding of sports and never refused a command. After
all, he is an endurance horse.
His name is GAZAL.*

**When he gallops, he humiliates the lightning.**

Horse of the Sahara by E. Daumas, 1863

Photo by: Mark Dees

HCC Gazal+/ at Squaw Valley the day before the 1985 Tevis Cup
Ride.

## CHAPTER FIFTEEN

# The Pursuit of Happiness

*There is no secret so close as that*
*between a rider and his horse.*

Robert Smith Surtees

Thinking about Gazal, I was drawn into considerable discussion on Ridecamp[1] on the Internet about what makes a great horse. People discussed the length of certain leg bones of the horse, the type of feed fed, the length of training rides, what color the hooves were and other factors. I thought they left out the most important quality—the heart of the horse. Not its size, or condition, but something that can't be measured quantitatively. And so I entered the discussion with the following:

> I think there is a dimension in regards to endurance success that has not been discussed in the posts of the last two weeks that have been the best thing we have had, discussions with real substance. I refer to the gifted horses, the Michael Jordans of the horse kingdom. They are born, not made.
>
> Many well known endurance riders can lay their claim to fame at the door of Lady Luck. They stumbled onto the gifted horse.

BUT, give credit due. They knew what to do when the raw materials came their way. The homework, the mental attitude, the dedication, the attention to detail, combined with the gifted horse, put them at the top.

I do not feel that there can ever be a blanket rule of how to train, how many hours, at what speed, at what altitude, how many days a week, how many miles at the trot or gallop. Individual horses vary as much as individual people. Horses are not born equal and some arrive on earth with the gene structure arranged so that they have more stamina than the average; they have more heart than the average; they are sounder than the average; they are less prone to illnesses and injury; they thrive on hard work that will break other horses down. It is up to the savvy rider to figure out how much is enough and how much is too much. When you figure out that equation and it all fits together, you have a world champion, a Tevis or Haggin Cup winner, a mileage champion. Natural talent is a God-given plus in our sport and while the equine klutz may, with arduous and disciplined training, become a good endurance horse, he needs that extra special something he was born with to become a great horse. The records of the Tevis Cup Ride (the one with the longest file of records) were made before electrolytes, DMG, heart monitors or massage therapy came to our sport. They were set by horses with awesome natural talent who sometimes rose to the top in spite of their riders. This is not meant to be argumentative with the posts of the last several weeks, which have been the best, the most informative and the most thought provoking of anything seen on this Internet forum. I throw this subject in as an extra part of the equation that has not been brought up in depth. I hope it will stir up some more great discussions. I appreciate so much the recent input on this forum.

It cannot help but stimulate us all to become more thoughtful and better and more compassionate endurance riders.

It did stir up some interest and the consensus seemed to be that I had neglected to mention that great athletes train like crazy ALL the time. In response I wrote the following:

Yes, the great athletes are great because they train like crazy, but only one out of a thousand 'would-be' greats rises to the top even though many might train at the same intensity. The difference is desire with which some are gifted. What I meant by the heart of the horse might better be explained as what is between the ears, or, the mind of the horse, which cannot be measured. In long-distance riding there can be no greater thrill than to point your horse at a mountain and have him want to climb that mountain as much as you do. There can be no greater thrill than crossing a finish line of a 100-mile ride with a horse who still has a tank full of gas. It is the ultimate emotional award that can erase 100 miles of heat, cold, hunger and fatigue and leave you walking on air. The average and typical endurance horse needs a little nudge in the ribs occasionally and the encouragement of his best buddy or other horses on the trail. The shining stars can stir our souls because the momentum comes from within. This can be, but is not necessarily, competitive desire. It is just pure and plain unmitigated joy in their work.

Their enthusiasm is not the adrenaline rush of a stampede start, (it is still there miles down the trail) or because they are crammed full of high powered supplements. It appears to be a self induced excitement that doesn't quit. Maybe it is the challenge. I really don't know the right word. The rider senses the horse's enthusiasm. It is contagious and then rider and horse feed off of each other.

There is an indefinable essence, an utter grace, that separates great horses from good horses. There are hundreds of the latter, but few that, setting all emotions aside, can honestly be called great. Four endurance horses that come to mind are Wendell Robie's stallion, Siri, who lit up the arena at the finish line; Ed Johnson's Bezatal who took a stroll in the park on Tevis Cup day and just happened to get there first; Donna Fitzgerald's Witezarif who flowed like water over a rock; and, of course, Becky Hart's Rio who at age 20 continues to amaze us all. And I will add a fifth—my Gazal, who was much too proud to ever give less than his best.

These horses set us on fire and make total endurance junkies of us all. The fondest wish I can make for my fellow endurance riders is that one of these special horses crosses your path just once in your lifetime. When he does, you will know it and it will be magic.

Gazal's love for the life his rider had chosen him to lead made me think about other horses I had owned. Some fulfilled my needs and some did not. Their happiness was as important as mine. In 1995 I was asked to give a talk to the riders gathered at the Fireworks Fifty Ride. It was the night before their annual 50-mile ride and I decided to emphasize that the differences between horses are as great as those between people. I titled it:

*"The Pursuit of Happiness—For The Horse."*

This will be fairly brief because I know you all have water bottles to fill, fanny packs to stuff and friends with whom you wish to talk. My topic is LIFE, LIBERTY AND THE PURSUIT OF HAPPINESS—for the horse.

The horse, when domesticated gave up his liberty to meet the demands of man, the master. He has become the slave, in exchange for which he usually gets two meals a day, and the other necessities. But it is his pursuit of happiness that I want to talk about for I feel that horses are entitled to happiness as much as we are. All we can do to help them in that pursuit makes us better human beings.

To explain what I mean by the PURSUIT OF HAPPINESS for horses, I am going to use as subjects four horses with whom I have been closely associated. My point is to illustrate to you that horses have as many personalities as people and, the longer we associate with them, the easier it is to see that they achieve a fair amount of happiness. I do not believe that every 7-year-old Arabian gelding was cut out to be an endurance horse any more than I feel that all people are cut out to be endurance riders.

Some of you know Gazal. Gazal the beautiful. Gazal the elegant. Gazal the proud. Gazal the faint-of-heart. Gazal in his youth had infinite athletic ability and there was seldom a horse he could not catch or with which he could not stay. He never really took a deep breath in 8,000 miles of competition. But pass another horse? Not if he could help it! Gazal lacked boldness and he could pull alongside another horse, but if he was as much as half a length in front, he ran stiff legged—with the brakes on, so to speak. He just plain wanted another horse to lead the charge and take care of the spooky stuff he knew was waiting for him around that next bend in the trail. He always nickered to the horses he caught up with, and if alone, would look backwards and call in hopes that another horse would appear. As a consequence, while Gazal had a lot of first places, he had an abundance of second places. He loved and needed companionship.

In sharp contrast was Myllany, the aloof street fighter. Myllany never saw another horse he didn't want to grind into the dust. If he spotted an unwitting victim ahead he would speed up, lay his ears flat, curl his lips to bare his teeth and fly by, quickly outdistancing the other horses. You never had to look back to see if another horse was coming. He let you know by a sudden burst of speed because there was no way he was going to let another horse pass. He won rides. He simply devoured the ground beneath his feet as though his hunger for more trail could only be satiated by more speed. This was his personality and his pursuit of happiness was beating the other guy. He was the opposite of Gazal.

Gatsby, a 7-year-old Arab gelding, was bred for endurance. Good bone, straight legs. What more likely prospect could you find for my chosen sport? Gatsby figured otherwise. I would get down the trail about a mile or so and Gatsby would balk. When nudged to go on, he would back up—rapidly. If circled he would edge over to a tree, or a drop-off. Our personalities obviously did not mesh and, before he destroyed us both in a real down-and-out battle, I passed him on to others. Do you know where this young Arab bred for life on the trails now pursues his happiness? In a show barn. His life extends no further than between his box stall and the arena where he has become a good jumper who loves his work, his owner and his new life. His pursuit of happiness is found in the security of a familiar place, not in the open spaces,

Ria is a 14.1-hand Hyannis mare, pretty, capable, but I never really bonded with her. My suspicions that we were not really meant for a long standing relationship were confirmed when she shied at a deer in the bushes and unceremoniously dumped me upon the ground. And then, while I lay huddled in the dirt, she kicked and broke my arm. I decided to sell her and she is here tonight with an owner, Beth Wachenheim, who really loves her, has worked faithfully and intelligently with her and they get along beautifully. She has certainly found happiness on the endurance trail, but with Beth—not with me.

So these are four horses, each with different and varying personalities. I developed pleasant relationships with two of them, Gazal and Myllany. Poles apart in personality, they were happy living with me and doing what I wanted to do—long-distance riding. Gatsby just never wanted to be an endurance horse and it would have been unsatisfying, frustrating and probably inhumane to ask him to compete in that endeavor. Ria has found happiness as an endurance horse, but with someone else.

My point is that I think it is foolish to try to make an endurance horse out of a horse that is not so inclined, And I think it is senseless to hang onto a horse whose personality does not mesh with yours. I do not think it is wrong to give up on a horse. I do not think it is right to demand of a horse something which he cannot happily and willingly give to you.

There are so many horses out there that truly love this sport. You can feel it and sense it in their attitude, their adrenaline rush at the start of a ride, in their desire to high ball down the trail in search of whatever is around the next bend, There are others who may perform under your insistent demands, but it is a master/slave relationship rather than one of partnership. I think a horse has a right to pursue happiness and it is up to me, and to you, to recognize when a horse is suited for endurance riding and when he is not. There is no greater thrill than competing with a horse that is happy doing what you are happy doing.

I know it is not easy to change horses. Bob says the first thing he ever learned about horses was that they are easy to buy, but hard to sell. I think that somewhere there is a horse for every rider and a rider for every horse and it is worth the effort to find the right one. I think it is a fundamental right to seek for our animals that which gives them a chance at the greatest happiness. This means the right owner.

I'll add one more observation I have made. It is perhaps a little bit irrelevant to this chat but I think it does contribute something to the happiness of your horse and, in turn, you. I ask you to talk to your horse. As long as you have treated him with kindness, recognizing your particular voice, its inflections and its nuances, is security to him. The surest way to switch a stand-offish, distant horse to a 'head in your lap' best buddy is by talking to him. When you are saddling your horse, feeding him, sharing a trail—talk to him. It sometimes seems that women have a special touch with horses. I think it is because they look upon their horses as children. From the time of a baby's birth, mothers talk to their children—while feeding, changing, tucking in for the night. Soon the baby starts to smile and find comfort at the sound of the mother's voice alone. Women seem comfortably able to transfer this feeling of closeness to their horses by voice also. Men sometimes find it harder to do.

I want to close with a rental stable sign I heard about. It went something like this—

WE HAVE HORSES FOR EVERY RIDER. . . .
*We have trail horses for the trail rider*
*and jumpers for those who care to jump.*
*We have cow horses for cowboys.*
*We have pack horses for the packers.*
*And if you can't ride, we have horses that can't be ridden.*

Have a great ride tomorrow with a horse who joins you on the trail as a willing partner in the Pursuit of Happiness.

Photo Credit:
Pat Mitchell

"The Pursuit of Happiness"
on Zayante at the Diablo Two Day 100 Miler in 1993.

## CHAPTER SIXTEEN

# When a Good Horse Dies

*There can be worse things for a horse than to die.*
*When we domesticated the horse, we assumed*
*complete responsibility for his life—*
*and complete responsibility for his death*

Matthew Mackay-Smith, DVM

"There can be worse things for a horse than to die," stated Matthew Mackay-Smith in an issue of EQUUS magazine. As with so many others, I have always felt I can tolerate pain in myself more easily than seeing it in others I love. This includes the animal kingdom where misery must be even harder to accept without other outlets to occupy the mind and help what must seem to be interminable hours pass. I have seen people so caught up in a book they are reading, or in music they are hearing, that they do not detect the phone ringing or other things that under most circumstances would be distracting. They also are able to put physical pain out of their minds for a period of time. Most of the horses I know are confined to paddocks and frequently without the companionship of their own kind. If in pain, each hour goes inexorably on with nothing to break the cycle.

I have strong feelings about allowing animals to suffer. If a horse is old, his freedom of movement restricted and there is no hope of his ever being pain-free, I think we owe it to him to put him down. I have caressed the newborns as they drew their first breaths and kissed the soft muzzles of old and tired companions as they drew their last. To make the decision that ends a life is not easy. Nature is far kinder than we. The sick, the lame and the halt do not live long. When a horse can no longer move with the herd, he is a doomed animal. But we, with every kind and good intention, frequently prolong misery through our love for the animal instead of honoring them with the blessed finality that brings death and with it, the termination of suffering. My friend Maryben Stover says "it is time when you realize you are keeping them alive for yourself and not them." Yes, I weep, and agonize over whether I did the right thing when I have asked that a horse be put down. I can prolong their suffering or I can bring it to a close with a simple word to the veterinarian. Euthanasia means 'good death' in Greek. It is the least I owe a faithful companion. I may grieve, but that is over my loss. The words of the Prophet Kahlil Gibran ring very true. "*When you are sorrowful look again in your heart and you shall see that in truth you are weeping for that which has been your delight.*"

I have lost two horses that had been my delight to broken legs in which the decision that needed to be made was clear. The first was Lady Kay. The other was Myllany, the street fighter of the previous chapter. My sorrow in both cases was over the loss of good friends in the prime of life. In these cases, I did not have options, however, and I walk away from the death scene without guilt. The accidents were not a result of my negligence. Lady Kay and Myllany both broke legs while in pasture and the actual incidents that caused the fractures can only be guessed. Did they make a bad turn? Did they trip in a hole? Were they kicked by another horse? Who knows? I suffered no guilt as they were put down, only deep sorrow. Their manes would never be there again for me when the world was unjust.

The routine that follows the death of large animals is fairly basic. The backhoe comes, and while I watch, the hole that will be the last resting place grows deeper until the now lifeless form, that served me so well, is rolled in and the backhoe returns the excavated earth. It is a long time before I pass the site without sadness, but gradually the day comes and the memories fade and it is all right—almost.

It is when I do have options that the agony for me is the greatest. I owned and loved *Marinera for 24 years. I learned more about life and myself while sitting on her back than I did from any teacher. At age 30 she was hale and hearty with mild, but not crippling, arthritis in both rear ankles. She had earned the freedom of the yard and I never feared that she would leave the driveway. Her daughters and grandson were nearby and at liberty she could wander from one corral to the other and touch noses with any of them. In the summer she spent her days on the ridge by the house where the summer breeze kept the flies away. She was not an old horse in demeanor, but vital and still full of 'brio,' the energy and excitement of the horse so prized by the Peruvians of her native land.

One evening, in answer to my calls from the barn, she pasoed her way down the steep driveway, mane flying and ears pricked for the dinner gong. She was as beautiful as in her youth. The next morning she was lying in our sandy ring and she could not get up. She had never let anybody approach her when she was recumbent and I was mystified. Her eyes were bright and she did not appear to be in pain. When the veterinarian arrived he said she had apparently lain down and remained longer than usual and, when she went to rise, her arthritic ankles hurt so she lay a bit longer. Now they hurt too badly for her to make the effort. He suggested an injection of a pain killer to banish the pain. He felt she would then be able to rise. However, he cautioned me that I would have to keep her on flat ground (which would mean confining her) in the future and give her daily doses of painkillers. I said "You will be back in a few weeks to go through this again and we will be repeating this scenario, won't we?" He said that would undoubtedly be the case. I told him that she didn't need that. And so it was over very quickly. She was put down. Was I too hasty? Is there ever a 'right time?' I've never been sure. But this vibrant and wonderful animal, who had carried me so many many miles with such enthusiasm, did not deserve to suffer. My instant decision still bothers me and I try not to reflect on it much.

Rumadi, my first Arabian horse, lived to be a healthy 27 years old, and, as was the case with *Marinera, maintained his vitality until the end. An extreme case of colic, something he had never experienced before, did not respond to the local veterinarian's pain-alleviating drug care. He pawed the ground as the pain in his belly increased and he was very obviously in agony. The only life saving possibility left was a three-hour trailer trip for surgery at the University of California's School of Veterinary Medicine located at Davis, California. Rumadi's chances of arriving there before a rupture took place were slim and the chances of surviving the surgery at his age were even slimmer. There was really no option in this case as there was with *Marinera and I never had to reflect on whether I had made the right decision. These two horses that rode so many miles side by side, now lie buried side by side.

Many years ago, at a Castle Rock Challenge Ride, a respected rider's horse coliced[1] and later died. While I was commiserating with the rider, she said "If you stay in this sport long enough, sooner or later it will happen to you." I never started a ride after that without her words ringing in my ears and have always said a little prayer at the start of each ride of "please don't let it happen to me." But the day came and the devastation it left in its aftermath can only be understood by one who has been there.

After Q-Ball carried me to my 20th Tevis Cup completion and

the first ever 2,000 Mile Tevis Cup buckle, it took me two years to convince her owner, my friend Maryben, that Q-Ball belonged in my barn and not hers. I had now owned her for about six months and the day of the Fireworks 50-mile local ride started out well, Q-Ball performing beautifully with no indication of impending doom. She ate and drank well as the ride progressed and easily met all the veterinarian established parameters as "fit to continue"—the yardstick now used to decide whether a horse should be allowed to return to the trail. It has also been adopted as the finish line criteria in order to receive a completion award. When a horse concludes a ride,the post ride check must show the horse "fit to continue" if the ride were longer. If the horse fails the check, you are disqualified.

Q-Ball passed her post-ride veterinarian check with flying colors. However, she did not want to eat and drink. Home was only 30 minutes away. We returned and I turned her out in the pasture with her buddies. She followed them about, seemingly serene, but still showed no interest in food or water. I put her in a small paddock where I could monitor her intake and check on her droppings. Her heart beat remained steady at 44 bpm (a resting pulse for a horse); she had no temperature and her respiration rate was that of a relaxed animal. She defecated, never looked at her sides, did not roll, paw the ground or sweat, or show any signs of the behavior typical of a horse with a stomach ache. Appearing tranquil, she seemed to be free of pain. About 11 P.M., about 10 hours post-ride and in my presence, she fell to the ground, then stood, fell again and regained her feet once more.

Justifiably alarmed, I called the veterinarian. Upon his arrival he treated Q-Ball for dehydration with intravenous fluids and stomach oil. She did not respond and he suggested I get her to surgery. Her pulse was now at 72, an indication of pain. An hour's trailer ride to a recently opened veterinarian hospital did not seem to cause her any distress and she continued to defecate in the trailer, certainly not an impacted horse[2] in my opinion. However, a quick belly tap showing bits of debris in the abdominal fluid indicated a rupture and the horse was doomed.

She was standing in the stocks[3] as the pronouncement was made. I asked the sympathetic veterinarian to administer a strong pain-killer while I called her previous owner. Somehow, it was important to me that I let Maryben know before the mare was gone. The vet replied, "Look at her, she is not in pain or she is very stoic."

I chose to think it was the former, and, in truth she did seem to be at peace. On the phone I told Maryben about the loss we were about to suffer. There was a long silence and then she said "It's okay, Julie." I replaced the receiver on the hook and turned to Rushcreek Q-Ball. I looked at the crooked white blaze that ran down the length of her face, the crooked legs that earned me my treasured 2000-Mile buckle and that had carried me 50 miles the day before and, once more, cried into a silky mane. I asked for scissors and snipped a lock of hair from her forelock, put it in a baggy for Maryben, and said my goodbye. She was released from the stocks, led behind the barn and a few minutes later the veterinarian placed the empty halter in my hands. Bob and I returned home and the sun was just rising as we pulled up the driveway with the empty trailer behind. Twenty-four hours earlier, almost to the minute, I had put the saddle on Q-Ball for the last time. But I mercifully did not know it then.

A necropsy showed the cause of death was a ruptured stomach, not an intestine. A ruptured intestine is not uncommon; a ruptured stomach is and is seldom seen by most veterinarians. The grandsire of this mare died in the same way. Could there have been a genetic weakness that the stress of the ride turned into a fatal weakness? Did she eat too much at the noon vet stop? Did internal parasite damage weaken the stomach wall? When she fell, was that the stomach rupturing? Why did she not paw the ground, roll or look at her sides as a horse in pain will? What did I miss during the course of the ride? There must have been, should have been a sign that all was not well. I have reridden that ride mile by mile many times in my thoughts and I still do not know what I would have done differently. The only hint of trouble was that she had become increasingly 'cinchy' in the last month and she squirmed when I tried to tighten the girth. I thought it odd, but did not attach much significance to it. I just decided to tack her up more slowly. In retrospect, I have to believe that this was the first indication of a problem that had been brewing for some time.

I will be forever grateful for that last good ride and Rushcreek Q-Ball's composure until the end. My 20th buckle, with her name inscribed on the back, adorns my midriff when I ride still. I smile when I visualize the little bay horse with the twisted blaze running the length of her face, the one with the crooked legs and the funny name. I laugh at the good times we had while silently acknowledging that all the wisdom of life cannot prepare you for the moment when you and a horse you love are separated forever. I think the ultimate respect we can pay our horses is to give them up when life becomes too difficult for them. If we truly love them, we do not let them suffer. Matthew is right. "There can be worse things for a horse than to die."

Photo by: Pat Mitchell

Rushcreek Q-Ball and Julie cross a grassy knoll with partners Bob and T+ Bravo on the Diablo Vista Ride in 1995.

## CHAPTER SEVENTEEN

# The Aging Endurance Rider

*"And for a moment,*
*this good time would never end."*

Dave Matthew's Band "Stay"

The aging endurance rider has to accept with unsought finality a couple of things in order to survive. Humiliation has to be tolerated with a diligently honed sense of humor. When I have to ask someone else to trot my horse out at a vet check, I am no longer embarrassed. Needing a plastic milk crate to step up on to mount my horse also causes me little concern. The humiliation I experienced as an 8 year old when Andy unloaded me before my wide-eyed cousins has stood me in good stead. Few things in life have made a more indelible impression upon me.

The aging process is not necessarily to my liking, but the alternative is even grimmer. So, with weary resignation, I grow happily older with my enthusiasm for our sport undiminished by age. Emotionally, the thrills are the same—the intensity at the start of a ride, the joy experienced during the ride, the soaring spirits when crossing the finish line, the exaggerated view when you are ten

213

feet tall and, of course, the gratitude toward a benevolent beast of burden who bore his burden well. It is the physical decline that has been harder to accept. At the dawn of the new millennium I find myself in a fifth decade of participation in a sport that has blessed me for so many years. I don't want it to ever end, but I do not live in a fantasy world. I am determined that when I climb out of the saddle for the last time, I will thank God for every moment he gave me to follow a path I loved. I have vowed never to become bitter because it could not continue longer, nor envy those who are still out there greeting the day on the back of a horse with untold extravagant adventures waiting to unfold.

I don't think any of us really think of ourselves as anything but youthful, and while you can face the mirror and stick your tongue out at it, your body sends other messages besides the gray hairs and wrinkles seen in the reflection. Slowed reflex action and lack of balance are the first physical indications that things are not as they once were. Translated, that means you fall off horses more easily and more frequently.

In my early endurance years, the 1960s and 1970s, I frequently crawled on horses whose backs I had never been on until that moment at 5 o'clock in the morning when a 100-miler starts. Both my 10th and 20th Tevis Cup buckles were earned for me by horses that, because of unforeseen circumstances, I had never ridden until the night before the rides. It took little inducement to get me astride if the alternative was staying on the ground. Marion Arnold, Wendell Robie's granddaughter, and her horse, Bandi, came to my rescue in 1979 and Maryben Stover and Rushcreek Q-Ball in 1990 so my goals could be achieved. I have successfully ridden two Virginia City 100-Milers on horses I met the evening before the ride. I enjoyed the suspense of not knowing how my horse was going to behave and having to figure out the personality and the capability of a horse new to me. Assimilating the sometimes difficult to interpret signals a horse sends demands attentiveness and the time usually flew by. With total abandon, I climbed on horses whose early morning mindless exuberance failed to intimidate me. I gave it little thought back then, and when I went off, which was fairly frequently, I climbed back on without hesitation. But the years have changed all that.

I am reminded of a story, the hero of which is our AERC's first president, Phil Gardner. He used to favor sort of high-strung jumpy mares and one day I asked him why. His reply was, "I like them, they are so unpredictable." Phil's and my paths did not cross for several years, but the next time we met on the trail he was riding a rather nice, sedate gelding. I asked him what happened to the spooky mares. His answer was, "I don't like them, they are so unpredictable." So there you have it. The older endurance rider seeks out a different kind of horse. Solid, bomb-proof, child-proof horses are what I want now, but with a flicker of spirit occasionally to keep me on edge. The adrenaline still needs an occasional surge.

What brought about the change? One word—FEAR. Fear of injury. It was not an overnight thing, just a gradual awareness. Youthful feelings of immortality have been replaced by a more realistic approach to danger. I have come out of some spectacular falls unscathed in the past, but now the loss of agility is accompanied by a dread of falling, and the fear of not being able to ride again.

So what do I do to keep going down the trail when I have two antagonistic emotions—fear and desire? I go with the strongest emotion. In my case, that is still desire. When the bulwark of fear overtakes desire, I will stop taking chances. But I have lowered the risks by being much more selective in the type of horse I will ride. The prancing and dancing horses that once set me up for a good day's ride I now leave for the younger set to enjoy. I want the three "S" horse—safe, short and smooth.

Another change has been in the need to excel. The original push that drove me was twofold—the thrill of going fast and the ego boost of a win. In my teens, *Dick* introduced me to the excitement of a running horse. High speed is more apt to frighten me now. Nor do I any longer care whether I beat another rider. A voice from within shouts "caution" and it is heeded. An occasional 'Top Ten' makes my spirits soar, but I no longer feel as though I have put in a poor performance if I do not finish with the front runners. However, I cannot deny that I miss the enticing satisfaction of working with a horse, putting in the needed hours of conditioning, developing the right mental attitude and then putting him to the test against the best in the sport. I train my horses less intensely now and no longer search for the flicker of stardom in their psyche that I once did, or in myself, for that matter.

Other changes include not being able to take care of myself physically as easily. In the early days I had no need for fanny packs or water bottle. Drinking only at the vet stops seemed to work just fine. The youthful body was capable of handling deprivation more easily. Now four water bottles are essential. In the long ago past I rode 100-milers from start to finish in sleeveless cotton shirts, through the cold dawn, the heat of the day and then the chill of the evening. It was just too much trouble to worry about a jacket. I cannot remember suffering terribly because of this. There is a difference now. My thermostat does not work as well as it used to and an inordinate amount of time is spent being either too hot or too cold. I now wear a long-sleeved polar fleece jacket that zips up the front. I can remove it without taking off my helmet and it ties easily around my waist with one loop that does not come undone. I have long known that the discovery of fire and the invention of the wheel were not the greatest achievements of mankind. Polar fleece and velcro are at the top of my list!

As the years accumulate, I have become more concerned about my horse depositing me upon the ground and then abandoning me to my own resourcefulness rather than allowing me to count on his four feet for survival. Second only to my helmet in importance, my security blanket is now a small fanny pack contoured to my waist which, when full, probably weighs less than two pounds. I start by tucking in a space blanket[1] and putting next to it some band-aids and a small tube of antibiotic lotion. Then I add a glow stick[2] to fend off wild animals or attract attention as to my location. I carry a knife with an easy to open blade and it is joined by a small leatherman tool of many untold uses. A whistle and waterproof matches are followed by a couple of leather thongs for quick repairs. Next I include some Benedryl in case of attack by 'killer bees' (I have been stung on five or six different occasions over the years) and some Advil tablets for pain. I tuck in some powdered electrolytes and water purification tables. I put in a few sheets of notepaper with a pencil which always has a broken point , but I have my knife to sharpen it. A Ziploc sandwich bag holds a Power Bar for sustenance. I add a hoof pick for my horse And then last, a lipstick because I never know who I am going to meet out there. So now my full pack becomes my security blanket. It is waterproof and it goes where I go—even if my horse decides separation is a good idea and sends me sailing through the air, homeward bound for mother earth as he, now burdenless, gaily gallops homeward for the barn. I used to clutch the reins when going overboard so I would not have a long trek home, but I have decided that if the horse is falling and off balance, I may pull him over on top of me. My experience has been that if I let go of the reins, most horses will stand by and wait for me to climb aloft once more. If, in a moment of perversity, they have chosen to put me out of their field of vision, I have lots of time as I creep home afoot to reflect upon my choice of pastimes.

The one physical demon which nearly brought my endurance riding to a screeching halt is being the owner of the world's worst ankles and feet. The latter are long and narrow, of absolutely terrible construction, and if I were a horse you would never buy me—weak pasterns.[3] About two years ago they simply collapsed. The tendons that support the many foot bones have expanded and contracted for too many years over too many thousands of miles of posting on a horse. They are like rubber bands that have been stretched too many times; they are not repairable. My feet were crumbling. I sought help.

I have found that the pictured items, when carried in a fanny pack around my waist, become an essential security blanket for this Aging Endurance Rider. They all fit neatly in the fanny pack shown. The items are a space blanket for warmth, hoofpick, leatherman tool, Band-Aid, Power Bar, whistle, leather thong for saddle or bridle repairs, Emer'gen-C (powdered electrolyte mix for humans), antihistimine tablets in case of stings, Advil in plastic baggie, note paper and pencil and most important of all, lipstick (above pencil.) I forgot to add a small tub of antibiotic lotion, waterproof matches and water purification tablets for the picture. I used to carry water bottles on my body, but I find then annoying and awkward. My fanny pack has three zippered pockets. I try to arrange the contents so that the flat items are against my back as protection against the sharper items that are in the more forward compartments.

When I was ushered into a local orthopedic surgeon's room, I was told it would be a few minutes, the usual spiel. To occupy my time, I studied the charts on his walls which showed examples of absolutely horrific feet and ankles. Misshapen, broken down, pointing in wrong directions, they were obviously extreme cases. After the doctor, young enough to be my grandson, came into the room, he studied one foot and then the other. He scowled. In an effort to make polite conversation, I cheerfully said, "Well, at least mine don't look as bad as the pictures you have on the wall." His sardonic reply was "No, they don't. They are worse." In his next sentence he told me that the tendon on the left ankle was about to rupture and should be put in a cast without further ado. This unexpected development was accomplished and, as I hobbled off the table and toward the door, I explained to him that I had to keep my horses exercised and it was critically important that this be a short term project. Looking at a near tearful long face topped by gray hairs, he gently put his arm around my shoulder, gave it a little squeeze and said "Now, dear, you don't really have to ride a horse again, do you." It was a statement, not a question.

I went home to a sympathetic husband whose life changed dramatically when he had to make up for my non-ambulatory status. Once the cast came off, I was still in some pain, even with expensive orthotics, and I desperately sought a second opinion. I was given the name of a well known orthopedic surgeon who specializes in keeping professional football players operational. His pronouncements were even more alarming than that of the first crepe hanger. After X-rays, ultra sounds, plus an MRI, he suggested surgery on both feet, which would include pins and screws with no guarantee of success. I was told to expect a six month recovery period after each operation. Riding? "No, never again." Now in a panic mode, I was becoming one of those frantic people who go from doctor to doctor until they hear what they want to hear. I wisely decided that what I really needed was an orthopedic surgeon who was also a rider and would be more understanding of the basic human needs such as food, clothing, shelter, and horses. I found one in short order and this savior and hero told me to "take some Advil and *go ride your horse*." Aha! The magic words! I was not through being ten feet tall yet.

But riding a horse was simply not working. I could not trot down hill more than a few steps. It was not so much the pain, which I feel can be put on a back burner if I want to do something badly enough, but the ankle support was simply too weak. My feet and ankles wobbled so much it was difficult to maintain my balance in the saddle. It was then I decided I would have to solve my own problem. I was spurred on by the encouragement contained in my mailbox one morning, an unsolicited letter from a doctor friend who was also a rider, Leonard Davis of Auburn. Having heard of my plight, he told me "do not let anybody tell you that you cannot ride a horse." He did not tell me *how* to keep riding. He just told me I *could*. And my dilemma deepened before I found the solution that in retrospect was fairly simple.

I switched from 2 1/2 inch wide English stirrups to 5 inch wide western stirrups with safety cages[4] on them. I can shove my feet in about 7 inches altogether and I do not have to flex my ankles. These stirrups returned me to being a hundred mile rider once again. The English stirrups and leathers gave my legs much greater freedom but the more restrictive Western flaps and stirrups have helped my feet. I do not walk easily or quickly and my feet get very tired. Riding down a steep hill is difficult and I must slow down considerably, but *I am riding*. Those last three words are eloquently beautiful to one who was threatened with never being able to say them again.

I have tried to stay physically fit by adding a couple of things to my daily routine. Since I can't walk very far, run at all or climb a mountain, I ride a stationery bike about 5 miles a day to maintain some degree of fitness. It is really not very far, but I find it unbearably boring even with the TV screen in view. Then, while waiting for the computer screen to light up, I have a ten pound barbell I lift up and down a few times to keep some upper arm strength so I can still pull myself up on to the saddle where the view of the world, under my concentrated gaze, continues to enthrall me.

In my estimation, modern sports medicine and technology have made endurance riding safer, but more difficult. I do not say it is bad, only that it loads the rider with more decisions and, as you age, you feel that fewer concerns are your goal. If one has never heard of electrolytes[5], as we had not in the '60s and '70s, one does not spend minutes, hours and days trying to figure out the approximate dosage and what is too much and what is too little for the horse. We are told that the minerals and salt loss by a sweating horse must be replaced if he is to perform at a peak level. At the same time we are told that we can do the horse real harm if he is overdosed, particularly if the horse is not drinking well.

If one has never heard of heart monitors, one doesn't go half crazy trying to figure out whether it is the transmitter or the receiver that is out of power or whether the electrodes have gone haywire. New to the sport in the mid-1980s, a heart monitor consists of two neoprene backed electrodes which are placed under the saddle pad at the horse's withers and under the girth. Wired to a transmitter carried in a saddle pouch, they record the pulse rate of the horse on a special watch worn by the rider. Once familiar with the horse's resting and working heart rate, they can be used as one of many important guides to assess the animal's performance.

I am told that at the race track they allow the horses' heart rates to go as high as 250 beats per minute, I could never push a horse that hard. In order to elevate my horses' hearts to that high rate, I have to work them at a very fast pace up a fairly steep hill. I visualize their great hearts, that can be the size of soccer balls, beating that many times a minute and I back off. At 180 beats per minute I become cautious and once it climbs above that figure, I slow the pace. It is terribly important to realize that a heart monitor gives you only one indication of a horse's condition. It does not tell you how tired muscles may be or how much the lungs are being taxed, nor does it reflect hydration or a dozen other parameters used to assess fitness. It is a valuable, but limited, yardstick.

If a rider has never heard of Easyboots[6] or some of the other innovative foot gear now being designed for horses, there are no choices except to shoe your horse the old-fashioned traditional way. In addition, feeding horses has now become a science with much attention given to calcium/phosphorus ratios, selenium content, protein levels and supplemental minerals. In the early days of our sport, you just threw the horse a flake of hay in the morning and another in the evening. If he lacked energy you threw him more and if he was too exuberant, you cut back. It was all pretty basic. Food fads are not limited to the human species and riders today are constantly trying to improve performance by experimenting with low-fat or high-fat diets, and varying amounts of protein and carbohydrates. To offer grain or to withhold it at a vet stop can start a heated discussion at any ride. Now I find myself changing my feeding program occasionally according to what the latest article in some horse magazine touts that appears to have some logic. It is exactly the same process we humans go through with our own diet. Sugar free? Low cholesterol? Fat free? Take your choice!

I think that horses are in better health and have more years of service because of these advances. My point is that life was easier for the rider at one time because there were not so many choices. Interestingly enough, looking at the records, our modern endurance horses do not seem to run any faster than they did twenty or thirty years ago.

In summary, my love of endurance riding has remained constant, but I am not a bit reticent in admitting to being more fearful. The insomnia and nervous stomach that plagued me before my first ride continue to plague me 37 years later. I still get the same thrill as I did years ago when we pull the trailer up to the barn to load it for an endurance weekend. I still back-seat drive Bob every time we pull out of the driveway headed for a new adventure. I seem to think that I must remind him every few minutes that "the horses are back there so drive carefully." Actually, the last time we started out he said, "The horses are back there and I AM driving carefully!" It is my most fervent wish that we have many more years of saying "the horses are back there."

## Chapter Eighteen

# Dare to Risk Failure

*To try is a victory, even in failure.*

b.w.

In 1996 I was asked by the Tevis Cup Board of Governors to give a pep talk to the first-time riders the evening before the annual ride. It was good therapy for me now that I was no longer competing in this particular event. I thought about my own emotions before my first ride 32 years previously. As I looked at their eager but apprehensive faces, ride statistics from past years told me that at least half of them would suffer terrible disappointment the next day. I wanted each one to feel special regardless of how far he or she traveled that breathtaking trail. Each one had worked hard for months, and maybe even years, with eager anticipation just to reach the 5 A.M. starting line. I hoped that the non-finishers would realize that they were just as special as those that did finish. Each one wanted this ride so badly, as I had in the past. My talk to them that day follows.

You are here today because you are about to embark on an adventure which I first undertook 32 years ago. It changed my life forever and I hope it has the same effect upon you because tomorrow you are all daring to risk failure.

Look to your left and to your right. Some of the people you may recognize and some you may not. But you are all kindred spirits and are bonded because each and every one of you have the same goal—the finish line at Auburn of the Tevis Cup 100 Mile One Day Ride. You also share something else. You have all dared to risk failure and for that you are to be admired.

You are realistic enough to realize that roughly half of you will succeed in reaching your goal tomorrow and roughly half of you will fail. About 50 percent of you will become totally addicted to this ride and about 50 percent of you will be able to take it or leave it. About half of you who cross the finish line will want to know where to sign up for next year and the other half will be glad you did it this one year, but don't need to ever come back. Of those that fail to find Auburn tomorrow, 50 percent of you will be more determined than ever to succeed in the future, and the other half will say, "This really isn't what I want to do." But each of you has dared to risk failure and that makes each one of you special.

Reaching your goal in a ride like this can hang on a very narrow thread. I have always thought success in endurance riding was divided into thirds—a third horse, a third rider and a third pure luck. The horse must be a fairly athletic individual if he is going to get the job done. The rider must not only use his head and have some riding ability, but must have also done his homework in regard to conditioning and health care of his horse. And tomorrow you need Lady Luck riding with you—no rocks with your name on them, no missed turns. Never stop thinking out there. Focus, focus and then focus some more!

I am really not a motivational speaker, but I do have two stories to keep you from getting discouraged when the trail gets too long for you or your horse. One concerns a man who tried and failed to complete this ride three years in a row. But he dared to risk failure one more time. On his fourth effort he finished in the Top Ten and he capped his long-sought victory by winning the Haggin Cup for the Best Conditioned Horse. How sweet it was.

Another is a story of a woman who 32 years ago trained her horse around a golf course, bought a new pair of jeans so she would look nice for the people, and at the first vet check was in tears with chafed bleeding legs. Her horse was lame and the pulse was slow in recovering. This was probably one of the most inauspicious introductions to our sport ever. She has since completed this ride twenty times.

My main reason for being here in front of you this afternoon is to help you succeed tomorrow and be proud of your efforts whether you find the Auburn finish line or not. In this ride, just trying is a victory regardless of the outcome.

I would ask you to remain calm, cool and collected, something I have never been able to do, and to realize that there is life after this July 14th date. If you can't sleep tonight, if your stomach is upset, remember, you are not alone. I would also ask that if there is ever any question in your mind as to whether your horse should continue, err on the side of compassion for the animal.

I have one more request. When you climb up through Squaw Valley and you reach the summit where the American flag waves, look back over your right shoulder at Lake Tahoe and then left to the mountain ridges you must cross and thank God for making you a privileged person.


When I went back to our camper for the night, I thought about the riders who were undertaking this ride for the first time. I was envious of them, but at the same time I knew I was sparing myself the agony of apprehension that for so many years clouded my world for days before the annual journey I mustn't cry for what had been, but rejoice that it had happened at all.

Any endurance rider knows that 'the best laid plans'—well, you know the rest. It happens a lot in our sport. There were occasions when the clock was about to strike midnight and I would find myself without a horse due to a last-minute catastrophe of some sort. As I have said before, horses are fragile. They have a way of going lame right before the main event, as though, in a fit of obstinacy, they had it planned.

Or they get the flu (yes, horses are as prone to flu as humans), or they go off their feed or develop a saddle sore that won't heal. The rider's immediate response is one of panic and frantic phone calls telling friends the sun won't rise tomorrow unless you find a horse.

My lament one year was classic endurance rider. I was without a horse as the ride date approached. My plight did not fall on deaf ears. A young girl I knew casually told me I could take her horse to the 1975 Tevis Cup Ride. She felt he was in great shape and we rode together one day and I agreed. She and her husband said they would crew for me as I did not feel at all familiar with the horse. Nusan's owner, Becky Hart, was show ring oriented and

Photo by: Hughes

Becky Hart turned her show horse into an endurance horse after his 1975 Tevis Cup Ride. She won both rides and received Best Condition Awards on Nusan

had never tried an endurance ride on him. He was a special horse for her and I wanted the security blanket of knowing she would be at the vet stops to assess the horse and perhaps spot something I might miss.

The night before the Tevis Cup Ride, Becky and Courtney Hart delivered Nusan, nicknamed "Boo," to the starting line which was then in Squaw Valley, California. I took his lead rope from Becky's hand and said, "If you think this horse can go 100 miles, why aren't you riding him?" She looked at me and said "Are you kidding? Me? Ride 100 miles? I could never do that."

Apparently, I must have made it look easy because when Boo and I crossed the finish line the next day, Becky decided that, yes, she could do that. It was the start of an incredible endurance career! The following year she completed her first 100-miler, the Tevis Cup Ride. In 1984 she won the Tevis Cup Ride on her beloved Rio and repeated the feat in 1988. The same year she became the World Champion Endurance Rider in Front Royal, Virginia. Two years later she and Rio became World Champions a second time when the race was held in Sweden. And then, two years after that, in Spain in 1992, the unbeatable combination of Becky and Rio became World Champions a third time—an unequaled record. Two AERC National Championships also abide in her list of honors. The Race of Champions has seen her cross the finish line first on two occasions as well as any number of other 100-milers. Her laurels include triumphs at many 50-milers and several multi-day rides.

So every time Becky wins another trophy, stands on another podium, or has a gold medallion placed over her head, I never fail to let her know that it was I who was responsible for launching her and for her many successes. But she kids me right back and with a twinkle in her eye says, "No, it was Boo."

There have been many notable people in our sport, with many more to follow, I am sure. One who stands out is Nick Mansfield.

Nick was a bellboy at the Mapes Hotel in Reno but also had a ranch outside of Fernley, Nevada. He liked cow country and rumor had it that he used to ride his horse, Buffalo Bill, to Virginia City on a Saturday night for a tall one and then ride home. The round-trip was about 60 miles. People used to question how he arrived home in the dark and he always answered with "Old Bill" brought me home."

When Nick and Old Bill joined Wendell on that first fateful 100 Mile Ride across the Sierra Nevada in 1955, they seemed an unlikely duo for long-distance riding, for both were heavy set. However, by the time I started endurance riding in 1964, Nick and

Photo by: Charles Barieau

Nick Mansfield and Buffalo Bill head over Emigrant Pass headed
toward Auburn and their 10th completion of the Tevis Cup Ride.

'Old Bill' were already earning their place in endurance annals.
Year after year after year, they always seemed to be able to find the
finish line in Auburn. Bill wasn't the most handsome horse ever,
but at the time he outshone anything else that had ever been
down that trail. He was the first horse to complete 10 Tevis Cup
rides and it was believed that no other horse would ever accom-
plish the feat again.[1]

Nick received his 10th buckle the year I received my first in
1965. The awards ceremony was held in one of the big buildings
at the Auburn Gold Country Fairgrounds and it demanded al-

most more of the tired riders than they could tolerate. The collective 'high' the successful completers shared faded rapidly as the temperature soared to well over 100 degrees outside. It was no doubt even hotter inside. In those days there were a lot of smokers and the air was blue and the dust of the Tevis Cup trail still grated in most of the riders' eyes and, of course, none of us had had any sleep. The ladies were expected to dress up and that included nylon hose and high heels. The calves and thighs that clung to a saddle for a hundred miles the previous 24 hours were not functioning at their best. By the time I put on 2 1/2-inch heels I

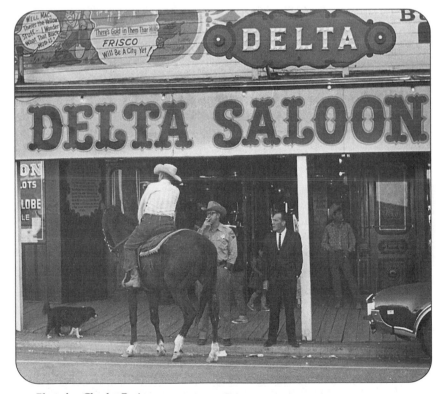

Photo by: Charles Barieau

Nick Mansfield in front of the colorful headquarters of the Nevada All State Trail Riders in 1969 in Virginia City, Nevada.

was barely able to stay upright, much less teeter up to get my buckle. My legs were chafed (we didn't pad the saddle with sheepskin in those days and we wore jeans, not spandex) and the nylon hose stuck to the wounds. (Dru Barner taught me the trick of getting into a warm bathtub with my stockings on to soak them off when the banquet was over.)

Dru took a lot of pleasure in deciding the menu for the banquet and she always chose her personal favorite for dessert, spumoni ice cream. She asked me if I thought it was a good choice and I did not have the heart to tell her that if there was ever a time for chocolate, this was it. Her selection was usually half melted by the time it was served and my voracious post-ride appetite was dulled somewhat by the appearance of the soupy dessert. When they finally cleared the last dish of liquified spumoni from the table, Wendell Robie introduced local political dignitaries who had had the benefit of a full night's sleep. The resulting lengthy discourses were not totally absorbed by the now inattentive riders sitting beyond the head table. Fatigue faded somewhat as the treasured buckles were handed out accompanied by Wendell's vise like grip of congratulations. Will Tevis[2] then presented the Tevis Cup for the first to finish rider to the applause of the crowd. Kept secret until now, the winner of the Haggin Cup was proclaimed by the head veterinarian and it was duly awarded. Just as we thought it was all over and we could escape to pursue the rest for which our anguished bodies begged, Wendell announced there was a special award. We all sort of rolled our bloodshot eyes around and groaned as visions of soft pillows and horizontal positions seemed further delayed. Still presiding, Wendell then asked Nick to come up to the podium. Nick was not terribly comfortable in the limelight, but he did as asked and stood by Wendell. Then they brought Buffalo Bill in the back door. They led him as close to the podium as possible and with Nick holding his halter rope, the two of them were presented with a large engraved silver bowl highlighting their successful completion of ten Tevis Cup Rides.

The glistening eyes in the crowd were a sign of the affection and the respect this man and his horse commanded.

Nick died in 1999 at the age of 93 and our beloved ride lost one of its greats. Nick was a true horseman, but most of all, a gentleman in the finest sense of the word.

The roster of endurance riders is full of unforgettable personalities—some of whom I am more fond than others. The most admired are those who give their horse's well being a higher priority than the finish line. Dropping out of a ride is more apt to bring praise than criticism. It means you had doubts about your horse's welfare and decided to take no chances. Socially and economically they are as diverse a group as can be found. They range in ages from young children,[3] being sponsored by their parents or friends, to a few who still are drawn to the scene in their 80's, not necessarily as riders, but just to 'be there.' Most are willing to put up with all sorts of hardships and deprivations to be a part of the scene.

The ambitions of some seek another level of the sport, international competition. Some don't need the upheaval it creates in a rider's life and they are content with less ambitious goals. Many riders line their walls at home with plaques and trophies attesting to their successes. Others throw them behind the seat of the pickup truck on the way home or among the old discarded tack back at the barn because the fun was in the doing, not the getting. Some bemoan their failure to reach the finish line on a certain day; some good-naturedly take their lumps and figure that that was today and tomorrow will be better. Then they start planning for the next ride with as much enthusiasm as for their current failed mission. Taken as a group, endurance riders are closely knit. In common they all share the joy of a day spent with a good companion. He is called "equus."

Photo by: Charles Barieau

With Lake Tahoe behind them, front runners Pat Fitzgerald and Neal Hutton crest Emigrant Pass at 8900 feet on the 1964 Tevis Cup Ride. Sixteen year old Neal was the eventual winner.

## CHAPTER NINETEEN

# *Once Again*

*There will come a time when you believe everything
is finished. That will be the beginning.*

Louis L'Amour

For 26 years I rode that extraordinary Tevis Cup Trail. My annual pilgrimage did not always end with success, but I never regretted starting the rides from which I was disqualified. To greet
the dawn with my horse and great expectations from atop the
mountain peaks overlooking Lake Tahoe was reward enough
for the hours, days and months spent in preparation. When I received my 20th buckle, my 66th birthday was well behind me. I
continued to ride other 100-mile rides, but this particular ride was
going to become a part of my past.

Why, if I am still riding 100-milers, am I not riding the Tevis? I
know why, and unless you have been there, it may be hard to understand, but the Tevis consumes some people. I am one of them.
I thought about it twelve months of the year for over a quarter of
a century—not just the day of the ride. I looked forward to it with

pleasure and excitement, but always tempered with increasing anxiety as the ride date approached. I worried. Was my horse ready? Was I conditioning too early in the season, too late, too much or too little? Was it an ego issue? Was I imposing on my family by pursuing my own needs? I remembered a quote of Douglas MacArthur's in which he said *"Sometimes we must make a choice between the roar of the crowd on one side and the voice of our conscience on the other."*

Why do I want to ride the Tevis Cup? It beats me down with hunger and thirst and discouragement, and yes, fright. And it raises me to incredible heights when my horse feels strong and the finish line is near. I am suddenly ten feet tall. I am special— never mind that 120 other people may have accomplished the same feat that day. For me, the Tevis was worth every minute it took from my life. It takes ordinary people and makes them extraordinary. It takes the housewife out of the kitchen and puts her at nearly 9,000 feet at 6 A.M. with the sun just hitting the great peaks of the Sierra Nevada which must be conquered that day. It takes the high tech executive out of Silicon Valley and decompresses him by sending him over Cougar Rock. It plays games with me in the moonlight. "That rock, is it really in the shape of a silver buckle? Certainly that shadow is."

My commitment is made at the moment I turn my back to Lake Tahoe and let my gaze drift west. It is an all-day commitment and frequently most of the night. It is a pledge I make to myself that I am not sure I can fulfill. It smothers me in self-doubt. But it also brings great joy, personal satisfaction and memories that will live with me until my last days—memories that I can share, relive and treasure—memories that are unassailably mine that no person or time can erase.

The Tevis Cup Ride does not affect everybody with as much intensity as it has me. Some people can take it or leave it. But those that can leave it, while probably better adjusted, will never have thrilled to it the way I have.

Why did I stop riding the Tevis Cup Ride? I was too much like *Marinera. I was never able to take the ride in stride. Each event became more important than the previous one. Sleep was difficult for weeks building up to the ride. I became unduly concerned about my horse's well-being. The ride very simply assumed too much importance in my life. The break had to be made. And possibly there was another deeper reason. I knew when I quit that I could still beat that trail. It was always the competition more than the other riders. I also knew that sooner or later it would beat me. Perhaps I, the aging endurance rider, could not stand to think of the finality of that inevitable day.

On several occasions I had watched in dismay as older riders continued in the sport when I felt they should have gracefully retired. I thought that time had come for me as far as this specific ride was concerned. I would continue to ride 100-milers each year, plus many 50s. But I firmly stated to family and friends that this particular ride was not going to consume me any longer. The Tevis Cup Ride had dominated my summers for years. For the first time in over a quarter of a century I was going to have the courage to say "no" to it. I learned, however, that it takes more courage to quit that ride than to ride it.

I thought it would be easy. It was not. I thought I could enjoy it vicariously by crewing for our daughter, Barbara, as she pursued her own goals of being the second person to ever have completed the ride twenty times. It was the next best thing to riding and there was a sense of relief at not having the pressure on myself. But as we drove up Interstate 80 toward Squaw Valley each year to follow the ride from the ground, I would look at the towering peaks of the Sierra Nevada, the great rocky outcroppings and the deep valleys. The yearning to be a participant again gnawed relentlessly.

The deciding factor to return to the Tevis Cup as a rider can be laid squarely at the hooves of a 17-year-old little grey gelding. In the fall of 1995, when Q-Ball left me, I lost the horse that was my primary endurance mount. In the spring of 1997 a friend, Pat McAndrews, said she was too busy to keep one of her horses exercised and offered to loan me C F War Hymn until I found a replacement for my lost horse. It was a fancy moniker to hang on a little grey Arabian who in reality has never been called anything except "Buddy." He was the perfect horse for me—small (closer to the ground in case of a fall!), cocky and a smart-aleck, sure-footed and above all, filled with desire. Probably no other ingredient means more to me in a horse. Some would call it heart or attitude. He is little—maybe 14.3, but I have never felt taller than when I sit upon his back and he pricks his ears and asks for the trail. If the rider and the horse both love a pathway, half the battle has been won. The rest is just polishing up with good feed and proper exercise.

In keeping Buddy exercised, I had ridden him in three 50-mile rides that spring and these events convinced me that he belonged in my barn permanently. And so, with little pride, I harassed Pat by citing all the reasons she should sell him to me. She reluctantly agreed and for that I shall be forever grateful. It also probably made me the only endurance rider foolish enough to place her money and faith in a 17-year-old horse whose prime years historically are between 8 and 14 years of age.

A second factor was a modern tool—the Internet. The Western States Trail Foundation, the sponsors of the Tevis Cup Ride, established a Web page. I was almost a daily visitor to the site. About a month before the 1997 ride, they started listing the riders who had entered, the names of their horses and all the information upon which endurance riders feast. I read it with longing in my heart, envious when I recognized a name. I lifted my eyes from the monitor to the pasture outside the window. With his head down, grazing peacefully, was my little 17-year-old friend, Buddy. Between us we had 90 years. Suddenly I knew we could do it as surely as I knew the sun would rise over Lake Tahoe and I would be there looking over my right shoulder at the Lake once again and over my left shoulder toward our destination 100 miles away. The pull was irresistible and, with joyous expectations, I succumbed to the return that I had known for a long time was inevitable. Les Brown said *"Reach for the moon. If you miss you will land in the stars."* Together, Buddy and I would reach for the moon.

The Tevis Cup ride manager asked Hal Hall of Auburn and me to lead the procession of horses and riders out onto the trail at the start of the ride. With Hal, Buddy and I led the procession of 200 horses into the darkness in the predawn hour of another Tevis Cup Ride. It was a place of honor and I was whole again. After a mile or so, we pulled to the side to let those who had personal ambitions of placing well pass. When we returned once more to the trail and into the dusty mainstream of horses and riders, I wondered where we would be at this time tomorrow. I was daring to risk failure once again and I knew the numbers were against me. Would I, after being blessed with a procession of 12 straight completions without a pull, be among the 50 percent who failed today?[1]

I was not without anxiety. At the pre-ride vet check the afternoon before there had been some doubt cast, and it clouded my mind. At the trot out, that longest mile, the veterinarian thought he detected a slight lameness in the left front leg. He called another veterinarian to help him reach a judgment. The two of them watched as I ran my little grey out in a straight line and then circled him tightly to the left and to the right. What they saw did not get worse on the left circle nor was it consistent. They said I could start, but on Buddy's report card, they wrote WATCH LEFT FRONT. This was a signal to all the veterinarians that might judge Buddy the next day to pay careful attention for a possible developing problem. From my perch in the saddle, I could not detect any unevenness in his gait, but I was realistic enough to know that at a start of a ride a horse's adrenaline runs high and can disguise minor discomfort.

It was not the best way to start the day, but I tried to reconcile

Photo by: Kay Allison

CF War Hymn, Buddy, makes his victory lap at the 1997 Tevis Cup Ride.

myself to the fact that though we were not starting out with a clean slate, we were in the ride! At each stop, the veterinarians looked at Buddy's report card and then gazed intently as he trotted out for the visual examination. Some thought they saw something not quite right in his gait, most did not; all agreed that Buddy's attitude helped them reach a decision. He was eager, willing and trotting freely on a loose rein. This was a horse that was having a good time and he was allowed to continue.

When we made our victory lap at the finish line at the Auburn Fairgrounds it was 3 o'clock in the morning of the next day. He was galloping and his white tail billowed out behind him. His eyes were bright and his slim neck arched. Together we had reached the moon. I buried my face in his silky mane and I was ten feet tall—once again.

## Epilogue

# *Not Alone*

*A canter is a cure for all ills.*

Benjamin Disraeli

The winds that so fortuitously blew through the Valley of Heart's Delight in 1944 with a free balloon at their mercy are remembered and appreciated still. Bob has shared 14,000 of my 27,000 total endurance miles during 56 years of marriage. He has joined me on endurance rides on four continents plus many adventure horse tours on two others. On an on going basis, we ride out our back gate three or four times a week. Anyone who thinks they have too many years behind them to start this sport should think of Bob. At age 83, he continues to accept the challenge of a 6 A.M. start and a 50-mile trail. He is the best riding partner imaginable. I make all the decisions on the trail; he agrees and nary an unpleasant word is spoken. He just seems to think it is easier that way. But he also enjoys telling anyone who will listen about his next wife. She is the one that will share a penthouse with him, have long red fingernails, wear high heels, go to fashion

shows and play bridge. During the times when just about everything seems to go wrong in the horse department, I tell him I
would be more than happy to buy the high heels, clean the barn-
yard out from under my nails, take bridge lessons and share his
penthouse.

Our sons, Rob and John, have been able to successfully fend off
the lure of the trail and have never really indicated the slightest desire to climb on a horse. Unlike some parents, I have never encouraged them or any of six grandchildren to ride. It has always
been a source of amazement to me that I am here today at all. I have
had some spectacular falls. I know with a certainty that sooner or
later the capricious nature of these animals we choose to sit atop
will put us unexpectedly on the ground. To see my own flesh and
blood plummeting to earth, due to my prodding them to ride, is
not something I could handle with much equanimity. If any of
them should come to me and beg to ride, I would relent, of course.
But they are going to have to want it badly, as I did as a child, before I am going to assist or cooperate.

I also believe that the love of horses is inborn in many people
and seems to favor the fairer sex. None of our grandchildren have
shown the kind of interest that I did at their ages, a period in
which I was so smitten that I frequently practiced whinnying
when nobody was around. Swimming, karate and running seem
to occupy Silicon Valley's next generation. There are no more orchards, fields of mustard or free balloons.

Endurance riding has given me many moments of joy and pride
outside of my own personal fulfillment. Our daughter, Barbara,
had no youthful riding experience other than six group lessons at
a riding stable in her early teens. Watching her decide to challenge
herself year after year on the Tevis Cup trail has been a source of
great pride for Bob and me. We did not have horses while she was
growing up and when she matured it was not in her childhood
memories as it was with me. The years I have not ridden the Tevis
trail I have lived through her vicariously, and I will continue to do

so in the future until the inevitable day when she also decides 'enough.'

Barbara's courage has been great as I have seen her repeatedly climb on horses with whom she had little familiarity and ride them 100 miles. On several occasions she has not met the horse she was to ride until the pre-ride veterinarian check the night before the race.

From me she inherited the ability to make a nervous wreck of herself for several weeks (actually months!) prior to the event. As with me, she has found it worth it. We have frequent discussions about our love/hate relationship with the Tevis Cup trail. We dissect it in segments and bad-mouth every inch of it—too steep, too narrow, too hot, too rocky, too dark. When we have maligned it from start to finish, we start talking about next year. It makes little sense except to those that have been there with us. They understand.

Barbara now has earned 25 Tevis Cup buckles, the record at this time. I do not ask her what her goals are, nor encourage her to continue. She has taken only three years off from the difficult challenge since 1967, twice to have babies and once after earning her 20th buckle. I think she had decided, as I had, that 20 buckles were enough. Then one day she said, "Should I?" I did not have to ask, "Should you what?" I knew.

I wait for her anxiously at the finish line as the successive minutes tick by and visualize where she must be at a certain moment. I pray that her horse, in a merciful mood, brings her safely home. When she comes off that splendid moonlit trail and into the lights and the crowd, I share her elation. We are both ten feet tall—still.

Barbara White and Tonto, the horse belonging to Nancy Twight, that earned Barbara 3 of her record setting 25 Tevis Cup buckles.

# *Endnotes*

## CHAPTER THREE

1. Rolling bandages consisted of taking strips of gauze, folding them into 4 inch squares, and then carefully tucking any loose strands inside so that they would not stick in the wounds of our servicemen.

## CHAPTER SIX

1. The horseshoer (or farrier) sometimes puts a heavy plastic pad between the shoe and the hoof to prevent stone bruises to the sole of the foot.

2. Circling a horse puts more weight on the inside legs and will significantly accentuate a lameness that may have been undetectable or only slightly perceived when the horse is trotted in a straight line.

3. "Tied up" is a term used to indicate that the horse's muscles (usually in the rear) have cramped painfully and he cannot continue.

4. Sound of limb means that the horse is not lame.

5. Dismounting, they grab the horse's tail and let the horse pull them up the mountain. I have heard that a horse, supposedly, can pull four times the weight he can carry so, once more, the rider is saving his horse's energy.

6. In 1999 this hour vet stop was moved to Foresthill. The Michigan Bluff stop is now only a brief pause while the horse's pulse and soundness are checked.

7. When I first started riding the Tevis Cup Ride there were no guard rails on the sides of the trestle. Hence the name—No Hands Bridge. There are some rails now.

CHAPTER SEVEN

1. An asterik before a horse's name mean it was imported from another country.

2. Spasmodic contractions of the diaphragm in time to the heartbeat are frequently referred to as horse hiccoughs and thought to be caused by an electrolyte imbalance.

3. The McCrary family decided in 2001 that, due to too many other obligations, they could no longer manage the ride. It saddened me, but their capable hands had done enough.

4. Many riders prefer purchasing a used saddle that has already been 'broken in.' New leather can be uncomfortable and stiff.

5. The first full moon after the June 21st summer solstice.

CHAPTER EIGHT

1. Both of these good friends were euthanized within the past year, victims of Cushing's Disease which robbed them of their vitality and made movement difficult and painful.

CHAPTER NINE

1. I felt my point was well proven when the first three riders to cross the finish line at the AERC National Championship 100 Mile Ride in 2000 were all heavyweights. Somehow they were able to compensate.

2. In the year 2001 the AERC sanctioned approximately 750 rides in the United States.

CHAPTER TEN

1. Horses are measured in "hands" with one hand equaling 4 inches. Hence, my horse at 14 1/2 hands was 58" high at the withers, the highest part of the back at the base of the neck.

2. A part-bred horse is one whose sire and dam are of different breeds. Breker had one parent who was an Arabian and the other parent may have been unknown. Technically he could be called a half-Arab as well as a part-bred.

3. A grade horse is one who is not registered with a breed association or who is of unknown parentage.

4. We were told that the Defense Forces frequently prefer Arabian horses for border patrol as they seem more sensitive than other breeds to anything new, such as where the ground has been disturbed in planting of land mines.

5. Race horses run anaerobically and are therefore very limited in the dis-

tance they can run as compared to an endurance horse running aerobically at a far slower pace for much longer distances.

6. Traditionally we think of 2nd place as receiving a silver, rather than gold, award. Apparently they preferred to do it another way.

7. In the year 2002 in the United States most rides require a pulse rate to return to 60 or 64 to successfully clear a veterinarian check. When I started endurance riding in 1964 the figure of 72 bpm was used. The lower pulse requirement is more protective of the horses. I have been told the pulse requirement has been lowered in South Africa as well.

CHAPTER TWELVE

1. Boojum is a name from Lewis Carroll's *Hunting of the Snark* involving an eclectic band of travelers.

2. Some Mongolians resent the popular term "ponies" applied to their animals. They are horses to them, although small in stature by our standards.

3. Horses are seldom gelded in Egypt. Stallions were common whether pulling carts or being ridden.

4. Leeches inject an anesthetic substance into their host and follow it with an anti-coagulant, thus assuring themselves of an uninterrupted meal.

CHAPTER FOURTEEN

1. The initials *HCC* represent the Hyannis Cattle Company. It is a common practice among horse breeders to preface an animal's name with a ranch name or initials so that people immediately recognize the animal's origin. The plus and slant sign following the horse's name represent certain honorable designations awarded by the International Arabian Horse Association for excellence in certain equestrian disciplines. HCC Gazal+/ 's *Legion of Merit* and *Legion of Supreme Honor* were earned in endurance.

2. The Haggin Cup was first presented in 1964 and was donated by Louis Haggin in honor of his grandfather, James Ben Ali Haggin, a noted breeder of fine race horses during the 1880s.

CHAPTER FIFTEEN

1. Ridecamp is an Internet discussion forum for endurance riders that can be found at *www.endurance.net*.

CHAPTER SIXTEEN

1. Colic is a sometimes fatal occurrence common in domesticated horses indicating a digestive disturbance. There can be many causes. It almost never occurs among wild horses.

2. A horse with an intestinal blockage, which brings the digestive process to a halt, is in serious and life-threatening condition.

3. Stocks are a metal enclosure not much bigger than the horse's body. Placed there, the horse cannot move about while receiving medical attention.

CHAPTER SEVENTEEN

1. A silver sheet which folded measures about 3 × 4 inches, but when open can be wrapped around a person to conserve body heat.

2. A plastic light stick about 6 inches long which, when snapped, exhibits a glow for up to 12 hours.

3. The pastern of a horse is comparable to part of the human foot.

4. Safety cages are similar to a guard rail. They prevent the foot from being caught in the stirrup in a fall which could result in the rider being dragged.

5. A salt and mineral mixture, usually in a molasses base, that is administered to the horse orally with a large syringe or as a powder in the horse's feed or water supply.

6. Easyboots are plastic boots which can be placed over a shod or unshod hoof to protect a horse from a rocky trail or concussion.

CHAPTER EIGHTEEN

1. Five other horses have duplicated the feat since that time. One quarter horse mare, Thunder's Lighting Bar, owned by Pat Chappell, holds the record with 13 Tevis Cup completions.

2. Will Tevis and his brothers, Gordon and Lloyd Tevis, established the Lloyd Tevis Cup in memory of their grandfather who was president of Wells Fargo & Co. Will Tevis, himself a noted horseman, set a record in 1923 when he rode from the Nevada State line to the San Mateo County Fairgrounds in $11^1/2$ hours, a distance of 257 miles. He rode Pony Express style, leaping from the back of one horse to the next in the relay.

3. The minimum age for participants in the Tevis Cup Ride is 12 years. Most endurance rides, however, do not have a minimum age requirement at which a rider can participate, but AERC rules say they must be accompanied by an adult sponsor until they are 17 years old.

CHAPTER NINETEEN

1. In the four years I have owned him, Buddy has been entered in 45 rides and has never been disqualified. I excused him from two rides when Bob's horse had problems and I chose not to continue. Buddy completed ten 50-mile rides in 2001 as a 21 year old.